AUSCHWITZ:
THE END OF A LEGEND

Critique Of Jean-Claude Pressac

Carlo Mattogno

INSTITUTE FOR HISTORICAL REVIEW

1994

Auschwitz: The End of a Legend
A Critique of Jean-Claude Pressac

This first English-language edition is published 1994 by
Institute for Historical Review
P.O. Box 2739, Newport Beach, CA 92659.

First Printing 1994

The publisher gratefully acknowledges the assistance of Russ Granata, who provided critical encouragement and guidance in making the publication of this work possible.

Library of Congress Cataloging in Publication Data

Mattogno, Carlo.

Auschwitz: fine di una leggenda considerazioni storico-techniche sul libro Les crématoires d'Auschwitz, *di Jean-Claude Pressac.* English
    Auschwitz: the end of a legend: a critique of Jean-Claude Pressac [Carlo Mattogno, translated from the Italian by Anne Sharp].

Includes notes, glossary, appendix, and index.

ISBN 0-939484-50-1
CIP 94-75562

Printed in the United States of America

Book gives specifics of Nazi camps

By Marilyn August
THE ASSOCIATED PRESS

PARIS — A new book with floor plans, photographs and letters found in recently opened KGB files recounts in horrifying detail how the Nazis built and operated the death machines that virtually exterminated European Jewry.

The Crematoria of Auschwitz: The Machinery of Mass Murder, published this week by France's National Center for Scientific Research, describes how a dozen private German companies competed for lucrative contracts to build and equip the gas chambers and ovens during World War II.

It tells how engineers, contractors, technicians and bricklayers struggled to cope with frequent breakdowns of equipment and constantly sought to increase destructive capacity.

The first oven, installed at Dachau in 1939 to dispose of "naturally deceased" political prisoners, cremated two corpses an hour. By the end of the war, a single crematorium burned more than 1,000 corpses a day.

More than 4,300 were burned daily in Auschwitz alone, according to the author, Jean-Claude Pressac, who once flirted with historical revisionist theories doubting or denying the Holocaust even occurred.

"I visited the death camps in the 1960s and didn't understand what I saw, especially since I was interested in the technical aspects of mass extermination," Pressac said in an interview published in the Paris daily *Liberation.*

'I never doubted'

"There was a time when the revisionists were the only ones to address those questions. But I never doubted for an instant the existence of the gas chambers," he was quoted as saying.

Holocaust experts say Pressac's straightforward, 100-page analysis of the chilling documents will provide irrefutable proof to combat those who claim the Holocaust, in which an estimated 6 million Jews died, didn't happen.

"The book won't silence the revisionists because they enjoy their notoriety too much and don't want to be convinced," said Nazi-hunter Beate Klarsfeld, whose New York-based foundation published Pressac's *Auschwitz: Technique and Operation of the Gas Chambers* in 1989.

"But Pressac, a pharmacist who studied chemistry, knows more about gas chambers and ovens than anyone," she said. "His work stands as the most complete reference book on the question."

It also will renew historical debates. Pressac claims that the systematic gassing of Jewish men, women, children and elderly men began in July 1942, not in 1941 as previously thought. Before then, they were killed less efficiently.

He also estimates the total number of Jews killed at Auschwitz at 800,000, not 1 million as previously thought.

His new findings are based on previously unpublished documents from the Bauleitung SS, the organization in charge of death-camp construction for the Nazis.

The documents were taken to Moscow by triumphant Soviet

Camps

troops after the war and put in the archives of the KGB, the former Soviet secret police.

Recently opened by the Russian government, the files contain two-thirds of the Bauleitung SS archives.

The remaining documents were left behind and are now in the Auschwitz museum in Poland.

Nazis secretive

Uncovering the mechanics of Nazi mass murder took Pressac more than 15 years. The Nazis were secretive about their use of deadly Zyklon-B gas and destroyed most of the crematoriums and gas chambers when defeat seemed certain.

Working like a detective, Pressac found countless "smoking guns," including a letter asking the Topf company, which furnished ovens for many German death camps, to heat, not cool, underground morgues.

Based on written requests to put in new, airtight doors and his knowledge that Zyklon-B gas became toxic at 80 degrees, Pressac concluded that the morgue was turned into a gas chamber that could kill hundreds of people at a time.

CAMPS/A9

The Daily Breeze, (Torrance, Calif.), Saturday, October 2, 1993, p. 1

Contents

Tables

About the Author

Carlo Mattogno in his studio

Carlo Mattogno was born in 1951 in the Umbrian provincial town of Orvietto Italy. He has had a broad as well as a specialized education ranging from the classics to the military. His Greek and Latin studies were followed by university work in philosphy as well as Oriental and religious studies, and while serving in the Italian army he attended three military schools. Today he is an accomplished linguist, researcher, and is a specialist in textual analysis.

It was in 1979 that Carlo Mattogno began dedicating himself to the discipline of historical revisionism. In

Europe, he has been associated with the French journal *Annales d'Histoire Revisionniste,* while in America, Carlo Mattogno has been a member of the Editorial Advisory Committee of *The Journal of Historical Review,* issued bi-monthly by this book's publisher. One of his books, *Il Rapporto Gerstein: Anatomia di un Falso* was reviewed and several of his writings have been published in English translation in the IHR *Journal.*

Among his hobbies are mountain climbing, cycling, and body building. Carlo Mattogno makes his home with his family in suburban Rome, Italy.

Publisher's Note

Numerous writings by Carlo Mattogno have appeared over the years in *The Journal of Historical Review*, which is issued six times yearly by this book's publisher.

Mattogno's detailed essay, "The Myth of the Extermination of the Jews," appeared in two parts in subsequent issues of the *Journal*: Summer 1988 (Vol. 8, No. 2), pp. 133–172, and, Fall 1988 (Vol. 8, No. 3), pp. 261–302. This essay is a translation of Mattogno's book, *Il mito dello sterminio ebraico*. It also appeared in French in the Spring 1987 issue of the revisionist journal *Annales d'histoire révisionniste*.

Mattogno's essay, "The First Gassing at Auschwitz: Genesis of a Myth," appeared in the Summer 1989 *Journal* (Vol. 9, No. 2), pp. 193–222. This is an adaptation of Mattogno's 190-page book, *Auschwitz: La Prima Gasazione*. Mattogno's presentation of this paper at the Ninth IHR Conference is available from the IHR on audiotape and videotape cassette.

Mattogno's article, "Auschwitz: A Case of Plagiarism,"

was published in the Spring 1990 *Journal* (Vol. 10, No. 1), pp. 5–24. (This is a translation of *Auschwitz: un caso di plagio*.) Another article by Mattogno, "Two False Testimonies from Auschwitz," appeared in this same Spring 1990 issue (Vol. 10, No. 1), pp. 25–47.

A critical response by Mattogno, "Jean-Claude Pressac and the War Refugee Board Report," appeared in the Winter 1990-91 *Journal* (Vol. 10, No. 4), pp. 461–485.

In addition, Mattogno's 1985 book, *Il Rapporto Gerstein: Anatomia di un Falso* ("The Gerstein Report: Anatomy of a Fraud"), was reviewed by Robert Hall in the Spring 1986 *Journal* (Vol. 7, No. 1), pp. 115–119. Also, a notice describing two books by Mattogno, *Auschwitz: La Prima Gasazione* and *La Soluzione Finale*, appeared in the July-August 1993 *Journal*, p. 25.

Carlo Mattogno is not, of course, the only scholar to respond critically to Pressac's writings, which have been widely praised as "definitive" responses to the revisionist challenge to the Holocaust extermination story. A number of revisionist writers have critically examined Pressac's arguments in reviews and essays published in the IHR's *Journal of Historical Review*.

A substantial portion of a detailed *Journal* essay by Spanish scholar Enrique Aynat Eknes, for example, is devoted to a critical analysis of an important 1982 article by Pressac: "Crematoriums II and III of Birkenau: A Critical Study," Fall 1988 issue (Vol. 8, No. 3), pp. 303–358.

Pressac's 564-page book, *Auschwitz: Technique and Operation of the Gas Chambers*, published in 1989, has been the subject of several detailed reviews and articles. It was first reviewed by American historian

Mark Weber in the Summer 1990 *Journal* (Vol. 10, No. 2), pp. 231–237. A considerably more detailed review by French scholar Robert Faurisson appeared in two parts in the Spring 1991 issue (Vol. 11, No. 1), pp. 25–66, and in the Summer 1991 issue (Vol. 11, No. 2), pp. 133–175.

Enrique Aynat Eknes also responded to Pressac's 1989 book in an essay, "Neither Trace nor Proof: The Seven Auschwitz 'Gassing' Sites According to Jean-Claude Pressac," published in the Summer 1991 *Journal* (Vol. 11, No. 2), pp. 177–206.

Dr. Arthur Butz, who teaches at Northwestern University in Illinois, provided a detailed analysis and commentary of Pressac's 1989 book in "Some Thoughts on Pressac's Opus: A Response to a Major Critique of Holocaust Revisionism," May-June 1993 *Journal* (Vol. 13, No. 3), pp. 23 –37.

Dr. Faurisson provided a brief, preliminary response to Pressac's 1993 book, *Les Crématoires d'Auschwitz: La machinerie du meurte de masse* ("The Crematoria of Auschwitz: The Machinery of Mass Killing"), in the Jan.-Feb. 1994 *Journal* (Vol. 14, No. 1), pp. 23–24. A much more detailed response to Pressac's 1993 work is provided by Faurisson in a 93-page book published in France in January 1994, *Réponse à Jean-Claude Pressac: Sur le problème des chambres a gaz.*

Other books by Carlo Mattogno

La Risiera di San Sabba. Un Falso Grossolano. Monfalcone: Sentinella d'Italia.

Il Rapporto Gerstein: Anatomia di un Falso. Monfalcone: Sentinella d'Italia; 1985.

Il Mito Dello Sterminio Ebraico: Introduzione Storico-

bibliografica Alla Storiografia Revisionista. Monfalcone: Sentinella d'Italia; 1985.

Auschwitz: Un Caso di Plagio. Parma: Edizioni La Sfinge.

Auschwitz: Due False Testimonianze. Parma: Edizioni La Sfinge.

Auschwitz: Le "Confessioni" di Höss. Parma: Edizioni La Sfinge.

Wellers e I "Gasati" di Auschwitz. Parma: Edizioni La Sfinge.

Come Si Falsifica La Storia: Saul Friedländer e Il "Rapporto" Gerstein. Parma: Edizioni La Sfinge.

"Medico Ad Auschwitz": Problemi e Polemiche. Parma: Edizioni La Sfinge.

La Soluzione Finale. Problemi e Polemiche. Padova: Edizioni di Ar; 1993.

Auschwitz: La Prima Gasazione. Padova: Edizioni di Ar.

Chapter One

Jean-Claude Pressac

Jean-Claude Pressac is the author of a large-format book on the Auschwitz-Birkenau complex entitled *Auschwitz: Technique and Operation of the Gas Chambers*, published in 1989 by the Beate Klarsfeld Foundation, 515 Madison Avenue, New York, NY 10022. That work, which was acclaimed at the time of its publication as the definitive proof of the existence of homicidal gas chambers at Auschwitz-Birkenau, brought Pressac praise as *spécialiste incontesté des recherches sur les techniques de l'extermination nazie* ("unquestionable specialist in the research of Nazi extermination techniques") and as *expert incontesté, sinon unique* ("unquestionable expert, if not unique")[1] in this field.

But to the expert eye Pressac evinces a surprising ignorance of the chemical-physical properties of Zyklon B and its use for the purpose of disinfestation, as well as the structure and functioning of crematory ovens.[2] This double incompetence in the two essential aspects of the problem inevitably led Pressac to unfounded conclusions in his 1989 work. Despite this,

his book is valuable for its considerable documentation and for a critical spirit uncommon in the traditional historiographic field, where, regarding the sources, a systematized theological dogmatism rules. Pressac should furthermore be acknowledged for his courage in overcoming, or at least attempting to overcome, the traditional historiographic methodology in this field, which he justifiably labels as:

> a history based for the most part on testimonies, assembled according to the mood of the moment, truncated to fit an arbitrary truth, and sprinkled with a few German documents of uneven value and without any connection with one another.[3]

That book provided enough arguments for historical Revisionism to be considered *crypto-revisionist*, evidently even by its own publisher, because it has been practically impossible to obtain.

Another book by Jean-Claude Pressac, entitled *Les crématoires d'Auschwitz: La machinerie du meurtre de masse* [*The Crematoria of Auschwitz: The Machinery of Mass Murder*] published in Paris, 1993, should have complemented his earlier book by virtue of the amount of documentation he studied in Moscow, particularly the archives of the *Bauleitung* (the Auschwitz construction management), which were left intact in the hands of the Soviets (p. 1).[*]

But in fact, reading his *Les crématoires d'Auschwitz,* one senses an uncomfortable reversion: Jean-Claude Pressac returned to the worst cliches of the worst traditional historiography. This was inevitable: In the 80,000 (eighty thousand!) documents at Moscow, and in the entire archives of the *Bauleitung*,[†] Pressac

---

[*] Page numbers with no other indications refer to: *Les crématoires d'Auschwitz: La machinerie du meurtre de masse*, by J.- C. Pressac.

found NO PROOF of the existence of one single homicidal gas chamber at Auschwitz-Birkenau. For example, concerning Crematory II at Birkenau, no "criminal *trace*" (Pressac's term) is dated prior to 31 March 1943, the date of the official consignment of the crematory to the administration of the camp. That is, to say the least, a bit strange for an extermination plant that was supposed to have functioned:

> as a homicidal gas chamber and incineration installation from [the] 15th of March 1943, before its officially coming into service on [the] 31st of March, to [the] 27th of November 1944, annihilating a total of approximately 400,000 people, most of them Jewish women, children and old men.[4]

Thus, for over twenty months of extermination activity in this crematory, for an extermination of 400,000 people, the archives of Moscow do not even contain one single "criminal trace!" And the same goes for the other crematories at Auschwitz-Birkenau.

This must have disturbed Pressac, who found himself in the difficult position of making these documents say what they do not say. This need explains Pressac's cranky methodology, which is characterized by his indiscriminate use of sources, and by arbitrary and unfounded deductions inserted into the body of the

---

† Pressac states that these archives were left intact because the second and last director of the Bauleitung, SS-Obersturmführer Werner Jothann ignored the "'explosive' contents of the documents" because *l'aménagement homicide des crématoires* (the fitting out of the crematories for homicide) was carried out under the direction of SS-Sturmbannführer Karl Bischoff (p. 1). But on page 88, Pressac contradicts himself, stating that Bischoff «avait pris la tête de l'Inspection des constructions ›Silésie‹, *mais gardait le contrôle de la Bauleitung d'Auschwitz*» ["had been in charge of the inspection of 'Silesia' constructions, *but retained control of the Bauleitung of Auschwitz*"] (our italics).

text within a dense web of notes so as to give the impression of coming from historical documentation. The connections among the various documents appears forced, and the interpretation of those documents is contorted to make it seem as if they support the existence of homicidal gas chambers.

Pressed by Revisionist research which demonstrates the impossibility of mass extermination at Auschwitz-Birkenau from the technical point of view, Pressac plays not only at diminishing the numbers of victims, but also with the intentions of the SS. The number of presumed homicidally gassed victims, which in 1989 was "about 900,000,"[5] of whom 750,000 were supposedly killed at Crematories II and III alone,[6] is here reduced to only 630,000 (p. 148). Both figures are completely arbitrary. Furthermore, the homicidal gas chambers have become "little" and thus of small extermination capacity. In effect, Pressac has been forced to "equilibrate" the capacity of the homicidal gas chambers to that of the crematory ovens. In his 1989 work, the ratio of *corpses gassed* to *corpses cremated* was much higher.

All these changes have naturally required jarring contradictions with respect to his preceding *Auschwitz: Technique and Operation of the Gas Chambers*. But this is unimportant to an author, who seems to accept or reject figures and arguments depending on his whim.

To complete the picture, Pressac has again enormously exaggerated the capacity of the crematories of Auschwitz-Birkenau as he did in 1989, arriving at conclusions which are technically and thermodynamically senseless, due to his apparent ignorance of essential aspects of cremation.

The subject of homicidal gas chambers has caused

Pressac no little difficulty, not only due to the absolute lack of proof on this subject in the Moscow documents, but above all, because the documentation on ventilation installations in the basement of Crematories II and III show undeniably that homicidal gas chambers were not planned, and were not installed. We shall subsequently see how Pressac attempted to overcome this difficulty.

The critique presented here is essentially based upon a scientific study of the crematory ovens, and of the presumed homicidal gas chambers at Auschwitz-Birkenau, which has involved over five years of research with the invaluable collaboration of Engineer Dr. Franco Deana of Genoa, and Engineer H.N. of Danzig. That work consists of two volumes entitled

> *Auschwitz: i forni crematori* [Auschwitz: The Crematory Ovens]
> *Auschwitz: le camere a gas* [Auschwitz: The Gas Chambers]

which are being published in Italy. The present work is a synthesis of these studies. The interested reader will be able to find among the citations of these two studies, many references that are not included in this critique.

The Crematory Ovens of Auschwitz-Birkenau, to be published in America, extends historiography in this field wherein researchers may find in that particular work references other than those appearing in this critique. The table of contents of *The Crematory Ovens of Auschwitz-Birkenau* is shown as Document No. 1 of the Appendix herein.

Chapter Two

Crematory ovens according to Pressac

Capacity: Suppositions

A scientific study of the crematory ovens of Auschwitz-Birkenau must confront and resolve two fundamental thermotechnical problems: that of capacity, and that of yield. Capacity is the number of corpses cremated within a time frame (reference: one day of activity). Yield is the relation between heat produced and heat used: specifically, fuel consumption. Jean-Claude Pressac does not confront either of these two problems scientifically, limiting himself simply to a series of statements as to the capacity of the ovens (which he erroneously calls "yield"), sprinkled here and there throughout his book. These statements, under analysis, yield the following arguments:

1. The mobile oil-heated Topf two-chambered oven which was installed in Dachau at the end of 1939 had a capacity of two corpses per hour (p. 7). Thus, the cremation of one corpse in one chamber lasted one hour.

2. The Topf two-chambered "Auschwitz model" oven heated by coke was of a design different from that of the Dachau oven. This was the result of a change in the first two-chambered Topf oven at Buchenwald which was originally heated with combustible oil, into a coke-heated oven, via the installation of two gasogenes in the rear (p. 12). Thus, the above-mentioned capacity of two corpses/hour does not apply to this oven.

3. The installation of compressed air *(Druckluftgebläse)* reduced the duration of cremation (pp. 13 and 68).

4. The "Auschwitz model" oven had a capacity of 30 to 36 corpses in ten hours (p. 13).

5. The ovens were used 21 hours a day, because their functioning required three hours rest (p. 13).

6. The three two-chambered ovens of Crematory I at Auschwitz had a capacity of 200 to 250 corpses per day (pp. 49, 80).

7. The two Topf three-chambered ovens heated by coke at Buchenwald (of which one was also adaptable for heating with combustible oil) resulted in:

   un rendement incinérateur supérieur d'un tiers à celui calculé à partir de l'expérience acquise sur les fours bimoufle (p. 39).

   [an incineration capacity larger by one-third, their calculations based on the operation of the twin-chambered ovens.]

8. The capacity of the five three-chambered ovens of this model installed in Crematories II/III in Birkenau was 800 corpses per day (p. 39) or 1,000 per day (p. 80).

9. The capacity of each of the two eight-chambered ovens installed in Crematories IV and V at Birkenau was 500 corpses per day (p. 80).

10. During the first experimental cremation in Crematory II on 4 March 1943, 45 corpses of *hommes gras* [fat men] were cremated; 3 for every chamber, and the cremation lasted 40 minutes (p. 72).

11. The "official" capacity of the crematories was as follows:

Table 1: Crematory capacity (Pressac)

Site	Corpses per day
Crematory I	340
Crematory II	1,440
Crematory III	1,440
Crematory IV	768
Crematory V	768

Pressac comments

Ces chiffres officiels sont de la propagande mensongères et pourtant sont valables. Leur validité apparente repose sur le fait que la durée d'incineration de deux enfants de 10 kg et d'une femme de 50 kg est égale a celle d'un homme de 70 kg, ce qui introduit un coefficient multiplicateur variant de 1 à 3, et rend aléatoires tous chiffres de rendement crématoire. (p. 80–81)

[These official figures derive from false advertising but are nevertheless valid. Their apparent validity rests on the fact that the duration of the incineration of two children weighing 10 kg each and of a woman weighing 50 kg is equal to that for a man weighing 70 kg, which introduces a factor of multiplication varying from 1 to 3, and renders all crematory capacity figures uncertain.]

Capacity: Facts

This reasoning is completely unfounded from both the technical and the documentary point of view. In this regard, we note the following:

1. The reference cited by Pressac is a letter from the Topf firm dated 1 November 1940 to the SS-Neubauleitung KL Mauthausen (note 9 on page 97). This document is a letter attached to a "cost estimate" *(Kostenanschlag)* of:

   > 1 koksbeheizten Topf-Doppelmuffel-Einäscherungs-Ofen mit Druckluft-Anlage, 1 Topf-Zugverstärkungs-Anlage.
   >
   > [One Topf two-chambered coke-heated crematory oven equipped with a compressed air ventilation system *(Druckluft-Anlage)*; one Topf draught booster system.][7]

   The oven offered is not the Dachau oven but rather the one installed in Crematory I at Auschwitz. This is evident not only from the "cost estimate" mentioned above but also from Topf technical design D 57253 attached to the letter dated 10 June 1940, concerning precisely the first two-chambered oven of Crematory I at Auschwitz. This drawing is published by Pressac as Document 6.

   Concerning the capacity of this model oven, one reads in the above letter:

   > Unser Herr Prüfer hatte Ihnen bereits mitgeteilt, dass *in dem vorher angebotenen Ofen* stündlich zwei Leichen zur Einäscherung kommen konnen.
   >
   > [Our Mr.Prüfer had already communicated to you

that *in the oven presented above,* it is possible to cremate two corpses per hour.] (Our italics)

2. As stated above, it is evident that the capacity of two corpses per hour refers not to the Dachau oven but to the "Auschwitz model" oven because "the oven presented above" is precisely that model.

3. The source cited by Pressac is the Topf letter of 6 January 1941 to the SS-Neubauleitung KL Mauthausen (note 25 on page 98). That the installation of compressed air reduced the duration of cremation is an arbitrary assumption by Pressac without any foundation in the text (or in reality). The text states:

    > Bei beiden Öfen haben wir berücksichtigt, dass die Generatorgase den Einäscherungsgegenstand von oben und unten angreifen, wodurch eine schnelle Einäscherung bewirkt wird.

    > [In both ovens the arrangement is such that the body being incinerated is attacked from above and below, thereby affecting a rapid cremation.][8]

    This letter refers to the two-chambered oven of the Auschwitz model, mentioned in technical drawing D 57253, and to the coke-heated oven (drawing D 58173) which was never installed, so that the "rapid cremation" (with respect to the civilian ovens) is nothing but the duration of one hour indicated by Kurt Prüfer in the 1 November 1940 letter. This "rapid cremation" depended upon the placement of the grill, made of fire-resistant clay, with respect to the opening of the connection to the gasogenes.

4. Pressac's citation from the Topf letter of 14 July 1941 to the SS-Neubauleitung KL Mauthausen is correct, but Pressac apparently hasn't the slight-

est idea of the meaning of this document.[9] This letter speaks of the incineration of 30 to 36 corpses in about ten hours in a two-chambered oven, corresponding to an incineration time of 33 to 40 minutes per corpse. These results could only be obtained under optimal conditions with the aid of an intake draft system *(Saugzuganlage)*. The installation's typical limit of efficiency for adult corpses was 40 minutes principal combustion in the cremation chamber, plus another 20 minutes of post-combustion in the ashpan underneath. This was altogether one hour, which even in the 1970s represented the minimum duration obtainable from gas ovens, as resulted from cremation experiments conducted in England.[10] The duration of 33 minutes (plus 20 minutes of post-combustion) could only be obtained in exceptional cases, and only for a short time. These data apply almost uniquely to the oven at Gusen, a Topf two-chambered mobile oven which was originally oil-heated and then transformed into a coke-heated oven like the first oven at Dachau with the installation of two lateral gasogenes (illustrated in Document 7 of Pressac). Because of local technical difficulties those data apply only theoretically to the ovens in Crematory I at Auschwitz.

The first cremation occurred on 15 August 1940 (p. 13). After only three months, on 22 November, the Bauleitung sent the Hauptamt Haushalt und Bauten in Berlin a letter which stated:

Der vergangene Betrieb des Krematoriums hat gezeigt, dass schon in der verhältnismässig guten Jahreszeit die Ofenanlage mit 2 Kammern zu klein ist.

[The past functioning of the crematory has shown that even in the relatively favorable times of the

year, the oven with two (combustion) chambers is too
small. (Therefore insufficient — Author)][11]

According to Pressac, from March to December
1940 there were 2,000 deaths at Auschwitz (p.
146), an average of 8 per day; thus, the crematory
at Auschwitz had difficulty in cremating 8 corpses
per day! The letter in question is part of the Moscow documents from the Bauleitung of Auschwitz,
but Pressac does not even mention it. His motive
in excluding it is easily understandable.

5. The gas-generating ovens heated with coke
    required a daily rest for the cleaning of the furnaces, because the residue from the coke that
    melted and adhered to them, over a long period of
    time, would impede the passage of primary combustion air through the bars of the grill, causing
    poor operation of the crematory ovens. From a letter by Engineer H. Kori at the KL Lublin of 23
    October 1941,[12] one deduces that the crematory
    ovens in the concentration camps were used only
    twenty hours at a stretch.

6. Accepting the data in the Topf letter dated 14
    July 1941, the capacity of a two-chambered oven,
    over 21 hours of activity, would be:

$$\frac{30 \times 21}{10} = 63; \quad \text{or} \quad \frac{36 \times 21}{10} = 76$$

so that the capacity for three ovens would be 63 x
3 = 189 and 76 x 3 = 228 corpses per day. Pressac
unjustifiably estimates an excess of 200 to 250
corpses per day. We say unjustifiably, because
from the very beginning, the data supply a maximum capacity for an oven with two chambers.

7. In a letter sent to Ludwig and Ernst-Wolfgang
    Topf dated 15 November 1942,[13] Engineer Prüfer
    indicates that the three-chambered ovens he

designed that were installed in the crematory at Buchenwald had a yield greater by one-third than that which he expected. Here Pressac, who normally confuses capacity with yield, commits the opposite error by using yield for capacity. In effect, the greater yield depended upon a thermotechnical advantage of which Prüfer himself was not aware (maybe because he had designed the three-, and eight-chambered ovens during his "free time" *(Freizeit)*, as he writes in a letter to Topf dated 6 December 1941).[*] [14] But this has nothing to do with capacity. Instead, Pressac interprets this as duration of cremation by the three-chambered oven as reduced by one-third compared to the two-chambered oven, which is technically meaningless because the theoretical and effective heat availability of the two-chambered oven was greater than that of the three-chambered oven (about 210,000 Kcal/h/chamber as opposed to 163,000 Kcal/h/chamber; strictly in terms of combustion capacity of the grill, 30 Kg/h/chamber as opposed to 23.3 kg/h/chamber).

8. But even if, for the sake of argument, the Pressac interpretation were correct, then it would follow that the maximum capacity of a three-chambered oven would be:

---

[*] The three-chambered oven, using preheated air in the lateral chambers, had an approximate yield greater by 1/3 than that of the two-chambered oven, that is a lesser fuel consumption by 1/3; in compensation, the volumetric transition velocity of the fumes in the central chamber was greater than their velocity of combustion, hence they burned in the smoke conduits. This, along with a careless use of the intake draft systems, caused the damage of Crematory II at the end of March 1943.

Pressac arbitrarily places the closure of Crematory II at 22–23 May (p. 80).

$$\frac{36 \times 21}{10} \times \frac{3}{2} = 113.4 \text{ corpses per day}$$

therefore the capacity of five ovens would be: 113.4 x 5 = 567; 567 + (567 x N)= 756 corpses per day.

But Pressac mentions an effective capacity of 800 corpses per day, which is then magically transformed into 1,000. Thus Pressac is not even consistent in his own technically errant presuppositions.

9.   Pressac does not even attempt to justify the capacity he attributes to the eight-chambered oven, which is as technically unfounded as the capacity he attributes to the three-chambered oven.

10.   The cremation of 45 fat adult corpses — three per chamber — in the five ovens of Crematory II at Birkenau in 40 minutes (reference from the witness H. Tauber) can be taken seriously only by those who have not the vaguest idea of the structure and operation of these ovens. First, the cremation time of one adult male corpse was an average of 60 minutes; second, the small combustion capacity of the grill with two furnaces, which was designed for the cremation of only one corpse at a time in each chamber, would have been insufficient to maintain a chamber temperature of 600°C (less than that required for a positive combustion of the heavy hydrocarbons which develop during the gasification of a corpse — at least 700°C) even assuming the simultaneous cremation of two corpses in each chamber; the simultaneous cremation of three corpses is *a fortiori* thermotechnically impossible.

11.   Pressac's reasoning, according to which all the

capacity figures from the ovens at Auschwitz-Birkenau are *aléatoire* (uncertain) due to the presumed presence of small-sized corpses, is in reality a simple anticipated alibi: Not able to understand thermotechnical phenomena with which he is forced to deal, he does not want others to understand, and therefore decrees that any solution to the problem of capacity of the ovens is "uncertain." Even here, Pressac is mistaken. We have confronted and resolved the problem on the basis of the percentage of babies and children presumed gassed at Birkenau, by their age and average weight. The result is that the capacity of the ovens, for the presence of corpses of babies and children, would have been increased by 20 percent. Moreover, Pressac contradicts his own assertion, because he accepts H. Tauber's story as true: in effect, that the cremation of 9 adult corpses in 40 minutes corresponds to a capacity of 1,417 adult corpses per 21-hour working day.[*]

Coke

Pressac mentions absolutely nothing about the consumption of coke at Auschwitz-Birkenau.

Ovens

Before explaining the question of the crematory ovens,

---

[*] H. Tauber states that the SS was annoyed because: "according to the calculation and plans for this crematory, five to seven minutes were allotted to burn one corpse in a chamber!" (Jean-Claude Pressac, *Auschwitz: Technique and Operation of the Gas Chambers,* p. 489). The testimony of H. Tauber is full of thermotechnically unfounded statements of this type.

it is opportune to rapidly examine Pressac's historical and technical assertions on this subject to furnish other elements with which to judge his competence and the value of his conclusions.

The Volckmann-Ludwig system crematory oven went off the German market toward the end of 1934 (p. 4). Pressac begins his "recapitulative chronology" with the Volckmann-Ludwig patent (p. 110). He even presents a technical drawing as Document 2, which has nothing to do with the theme he has developed, evidently only to impress those who exalt him as *expert incontesté* on the subject of cremation.[15]

The H. R. Heinicke company, holder of the Volckmann-Ludwig patent, at that time had its headquarters at Chemnitz. They installed fifteen other ovens of this type in Germany between 1935 and 1940.[16]

From the W. Müller oven of Allach, the SS deduced that a cremation without casket permitted a cremation time reduction of half an hour, and that 100 kg of coke were enough to cremate twenty corpses in one day (p. 6).

In a gasogene oven, heated with coke, the casket delayed corpse-water vaporization by 5 to 6 minutes, acting in a way as a thermal shield until breaking apart by the effect of the flames. Simultaneously, the heat produced by the casket, which raised the temperature of the chamber to 1,100°C, accelerated the vaporization process, therefore cremation without a casket did not take less time than cremation with a casket.

Regarding the consumption of coke in the gasogene ovens, incomparably the most important fact to be found in the specialized German literature of the time, is the cremation experiment conducted by Engineer Richard Kessler, one of the top specialists on cremation during the 1920s and 1930s. This experiment occurred 5 January 1927 in the Gebrüder Beck, Offenbach system oven, at the crematory of Dessau.[17] The results of the experiment, displayed in two thermotechnical diagrams, for each of the eight corpses cremated one after the other, were an average consumption of 29.5 kg of coke, plus the casket. These diagrams are of exceptional importance in understanding the operation of the gasogene crematory ovens. With the oven at thermal equilibrium (in a hypothesis of twenty consecutive cremations), the consumption of coke would have been reduced to 23 kg, plus the casket. A casket averaging 40 kg produced an actual quantity of heat equal to that produced by 15 kg of coke, therefore a cremation without a casket required about 38 kg of coke, and with 100 kg of coke three corpses could be cremated, not twenty. The "deduction" is evidently not that of the SS, but rather that of Pressac, and it is a very poor deduction.

For Pressac, the function of the intake draft was to:

> augmenter la quantité de gaz de combustion et d'éviter ainsi une dépense de combustible supplémentaire lors de l'incinération des cadavres ‹glacés›. (p. 29)

> [increase the quantity of combustion gas and thus avoid the waste of additional fuel when incinerating 'frozen' corpses.]

Here Pressac confuses the abilities of the Volckmann-Ludwig gas oven with the coke ovens of Auschwitz-Birkenau. Actually, in the gasogene oven heated by coke, the intake draught, impacting directly on the draft of the furnaces of the gasogene, caused an increase in the combustion capacity of the grill (the amount of coke burned hourly in the furnace), and consequently an increase in the consumption of coke.

In Crematory I at Auschwitz, which had a chimney 15 meters high,

> Koehler ajouta un carneau de liaison de 12 mètres pour obtenir une longueur de tirage de 27 mètres. (p. 40)

> [Koehler added an exterior flue twelve meters long to obtain an intake of twenty-seven meters.]

In reality, the force of the intake of a chimney is determined by the height and cross-section of the flue above the grill. The working formula given by Engineer W. Heepke in his classic work on crematories[18] is precisely $Z = 0.6 \times H$ (for a fume temperature of 250°C), where Z is the force of the intake and H the height of the flue above the grill of the furnace. The length of the smoke conduit can only have a negative influence on the intake because too long a conduit would cool the fumes excessively.

Pressac attributes the last page of a *Kostenvoranschlag* (cost estimate) by Topf for Auschwitz dated 1 April 1943 in the amount of 25,148 Reichsmark, published by R. Schnabel,[19] to the planned Crematory VI,

> fondé sur le principe de l'incinération à ciel ouvert. (p. 69)

> [based on the principle of open-sky incineration],

Pressac's interpretation (*à ciel ouvert* = 'cremation pits') is unsustainable because the document in question mentions:

> 1 gusseiserner Rauchkanalschieber mit Rollen, Drahtseil und Handwinde.

> [one cast iron damper with pulleys, steel cable and hand winch.],

and a smoke conduit infers a closed combustion chamber on one side and on the other a chimney; installations that would not be recommended for an *à ciel ouvert* (open-air) combustion.

Flames

Pressac has the audacity to accept the story told by various eyewitnesses of flames coming out of the chimneys (of Crematories II and III) (p. 91).

This is technically impossible. Any uncombusted gas emitted from the chambers would either be burned in the smoke conduits if there were the necessary ignition temperature and combustion air, or, should these two conditions not exist, they would emerge from the oven uncombusted. In the first case, completely combusted gas would be emitted from the chimney (particularly nitrogen, carbon dioxide, water vapor, and a minimum amount of sulfur dioxide); in the second case, only smoke would emerge.

Cremation Pits

Even the story of the cremation pits, similarly accepted by Pressac, is technically meaningless. The cremation of corpses in pits by the process described by the eyewitnesses is impossible due to the lack of oxygen in the lower portion of the pit. In 1871, the attempt to cremate the dead soldiers from the Battle of Sédan, by opening mass graves, filling them with tar and setting them on fire, resulted in charring of the uppermost layer of corpses, the baking of the intermediate layer, and no effect on the bottom layer.[20]

- Technical drawings of the crematory ovens made by Pressac contain structural errors due to his lack of thermotechnical knowledge. Here are some examples:

- Plan of the modified Dachau oven (p. 14): The connection of the two gasogenes to the chambers is incorrect (the products of combustion of the gasogenes were emitted in the posterior part of the chambers and discharged directly into the smoke conduit).

- Plan of the three-chambered oven at Buchenwald (p. 28): The connection system of the gasogenes to the chambers is wrong (the two gasogenes were connected only to the two lateral chambers; the products of combustion penetrated the central chamber through the three inter-chamber openings that were found in the inner wall of the lateral chambers).

- The plan of the *rustique* (rustic) three-chambered oven (p. 37) is a plan of the probable disposition of the two simplified three-chambered oven (p. 50): The oven only had one gasogene (the *Kostenanschlag* of 12 February 1942 mentions only one horizontal grill *Planrost*,[21] not two. The connection system of the two gasogenes to the three chambers through three connection apertures is wrong; the discharge system of the combusted gases is wrong (due to the draft of the chimney, most of the combusted gases would have passed through the point of least resistance, that is, through the chamber closest to the smoke conduit).

- Plan of the initial eight-chambered oven (p. 78): The discharge system of the combusted gases is wrong; the external chamber of every couple of chambers was connected to the horizontal smoke conduit through a vertical conduit placed in the wall of the posterior part of the chamber. Pressac places this conduit between the two chambers.

- Plan of the reinforced eight-chambered oven (p. 78): The discharge system of the combusted gases is wrong; the discharge conduit situated by the gasogenes (at the right of the plan) did not exist.

Chapter Three

Cremation Technology

Here we briefly review the results of our thermotechnical study on the Auschwitz-Birkenau crematory ovens.

Coke consumption

The theoretical consumption of coke in the two-chambered oven, according to the method calculated by Engineer Wilhelm Heepke[22] (the most thorough to be found in the German technical literature of the period), for an emaciated adult corpse, is 27.8 kg, and for a normal corpse is 22.7 kg.

The real consumption of coke in the two-chambered oven at Gusen, for the cremation of 677 corpses (presumably emaciated) during a cremation period of 13 days, on the average 52 corpses per day, therefore with the oven in permanent thermal equilibrium, was 20,700 kg,[23] averaging 30.5 kg per corpse.

The consumption of the two-chambered oven, adjusted to reflect these experimental data, is 30.5 kg per emaciated corpse and 25 kg for a normal corpse. The consumption of the three-chambered oven (with a reduction of one-third) is 20.3 kg for an emaciated corpse and 16.7 kg for a normal corpse. The consumption of the eight-chambered oven (with a reduction of one-half) is 15.25 kg for an emaciated corpse and 12.5 kg for a normal corpse.

In the following table we summarize the coke consumption of the single crematory ovens at Auschwitz-Birkenau:

Table 2: Crematory coke consumption

Type of oven	Emaciated Corpse	Normal Corpse
Two-Chambered	30.5 kg	25 kg
Three-Chambered	20.3 kg	16.7 kg
Eight-Chambered	15.25 kg	12.5 kg

Capacity

The average cremation time of a continuously operating oven was about forty minutes of principal combustion (in the chamber), obtainable with the aid of the installation of an intake draft system (data relative to the Gusen oven).

The average time of a cremation without an intake draft system (taking into account the combustion capacity of the furnace grill) was sixty minutes, as is evident from the statement by Engineer Prüfer (in the 1 November 1940 letter), as well as from the diagrams published by Engineer R. Kessler concerning the principal combustion in the chamber (considering the structural differences of the Gebrüder Beck oven compared to those at Auschwitz-Birkenau). Because the

Auschwitz-Birkenau ovens lacked draft intake installations (p. 81), the average time for a cremation (principal combustion in the chamber) was one hour. The
continuous operation of the ovens was 20 hours per
day, at the most. Therefore, the capacity of the single
crematories was as follows:

Table 3: Crematory capacity (actual)

Site	Corpses per day
Crematory I	120[a]
Crematory II	300
Crematory III	300
Crematory IV	118
Crematory V	160
Totals:	1,040

a. This is the maximum theoretical capacity. The existing documents show that the effective capacity was much less.

Supposing the reality of homicidal gassings, considering the percentage of small-sized bodies among the
corpses, as well as average weight as a function of age,
the daily capacity would have increased by 20 percent:
Column I. In Column II, we include the data from the
28 June 1943 letter which Pressac considers valid in
the cremation hypothesis of babies and children, as
shown in the following table:

Table 4: Cremation variances by size

Site	I	II
Crematory I	144	340
Crematory II	360	1,440
Crematory III	360	1,440
Crematory IV	192	768
Crematory V	192	768
Totals:	1,248	4,756

Because in twenty hours, the ovens altogether could burn (based on the combustion capacity of the single oven's grill) 23,200 kg of coke, the average coke consumption for each corpse — according to Jean-Claude Pressac — would be (23,000 x 4,756 =) 4.87 kg, which is thermotechnically impossible.

The reason for the crematories

The decision to build three more crematories at Birkenau was made on 19 August 1942 (p. 49), *after* Himmler, during his inspection of Auschwitz on 17 and 18 July 1942, had ordered that the actual forecast for the KGL (prisoner of war camp) at Birkenau be increased from 125,000 to 200,000 prisoners (p. 44). It also came *during* the terrible typhus epidemic in the summer of 1942, which caused decimation in the Auschwitz-Birkenau camp: In the male sector alone, from 1 to 19 August, 4,113 deaths were registered,[24] on the average 216 per day. In the third trimester of 1942, the mortality was 20.5 percent of the average camp population,[25] which did not exceed 25,000. The capacity of the crematories was therefore quite adequate for the camp population established by Himmler, and provided for a possible future typhus epidemic.

Cremations in 1943: The SS estimate

The *Aktenvermerk* (file entry for the records) of 17 March 1943[26] (mentioned by Pressac on p. 119) shows the coke consumption estimate for the four crematories at Birkenau. The operational time of the crematories is estimated at 12 hours. The letter indicates the combustion capacity of the grills of the ovens; therefore one is able to calculate the number of corpses that could possibly be cremated, namely, about 362 emaciated adult corpses per day. From 1 March to 17 March the average mortality at Birkenau was 292 prisoners per day,[27] which, in terms of coke consumption for cremation, represents 80 percent of the estimate by the SS. This means that this estimate was calculated on the basis of the actual average mortality plus a 20 percent security margin. Because the average of the presumed gassed according to the *Kalendarium of Auschwitz* during this period is about 1,100 per day, if the story of the homicidal gas chambers were true, during this period there would have been an average daily death toll of about 1,400, approximately four times the actual estimate of the SS.

Cremations in 1943: Coke consumption

From 1 March to 25 October 1943 a total of 641.5 tons of coke was supplied to the crematories of Auschwitz-Birkenau.[28] In this period, the number of natural deaths among the prisoners was about 27,300, that of the presumed gassed about 118,300,[29] thus altogether about 145,600. For the prisoners deceased of natural causes, there results an average coke availability of (641,500 : 27,300 =) 23.5 kg per corpse, a figure which is quite compatible with the consumption of the ovens. For the presumed homicidally gassed, plus the prisoners deceased of natural causes, instead there results an availability of (641,000 :145,600 =) 4.4 kg, which is thermotechnically impossible.

The estimate of the SS of 17 March 1943, and the quantity of coke supplied to the crematories from March to October 1943, demonstrate that the crematories cremated *only* the corpses of the registered prisoners deceased of natural causes and that, consequently, there was no mass homicidal gassing.

Crematory capacity in 1943

From 14 March to 25 October 1943, the crematories at Birkenau were able to function only for a total of about 400 days. The maximum number of cremations theoretically possible (with the capacities taking into account corpses of babies and children) is about 100,000, but the number of corpses to be cremated (presumed homicidally gassed plus registered prisoners) is about 142,000. Thus, the cremation capability of the crematories rendered the cremation of presumed homicidally gassed prisoners impossible; therefore, there was no mass homicidal gassing.

In *Auschwitz: Technique and Operation of the Gas Chambers,* Jean-Claude Pressac states that from April to October 1943 the crematories at Birkenau cremated 165,000 to 215,000 corpses with 497 tons of coke,[30] which means that for him it was possible to cremate a corpse with an average of 2.6 kg of coke!

According to Rudolf Höss, Crematories II and III

could cremate 2,000 corpses per day, Crematories IV and V, 1,500 per day.[31] Hence the average consumption of coke per corpse was respectively 3.5 kg and 1.8 kg!

The longevity of crematory walls

In his 1989 book, Jean-Claude Pressac furnishes the following numbers of corpses cremated at Auschwitz-Birkenau:

Table 5: Cremations at Auschwitz-Birkenau[a]

Site	Cremations
Crematory I	10,000[32]
Crematory II	400,000[33]
Crematory III	350,000[34]
Crematory IV	6,000[35]
Crematory V	15,000[36]
Subtotal:	781,000

Cremation Pit 1942	107,000[37]
Cremation Pit 1944	50,000[38]
Subtotal:	157,000
Total:	938,000

a. These numbers refer exclusively to those presumed homicidally gassed and do not include the corpses of the registered prisoners who died of natural causes.

In his 1993 book, Jean-Claude Pressac reduces the

number of presumed homicidally gassed to 630,000, and furnishes a total general death toll of 775,000, rounded off to approximately 800,000 (p. 148).

This revision of the number of those alleged to have been gassed has no relation to the Moscow documents studied by Pressac. The reduction is dictated exclusively by his realization that the Birkenau crematories in 1943 (and mostly in Spring and Summer of 1944: see No.8) could not have cremated the corpses of the presumed homicidally gassed even with the inflated capacity numbers he adopted. To eliminate the contradiction, he decrees that the number of the deported brought to Auschwitz-Birkenau at this time according to the *Auschwitz Kalendarium* (about 53,000) and, consequently, of the presumed homicidally gassed (about 42,000) is excessive (p. 147). Now Pressac, on the basis of simple conjecture, expects to "correct" in one little page, the recent study by Franciszek Piper on the number of victims of Auschwitz-Birkenau,[39] which is the most in-depth and documented Exterminationist work, compiled from the documents in possession of the museum of Auschwitz. Therefore, from the point of view of the supporters of the reality of homicidal gas chambers, the reference work remains that of Piper, and the affirmations of Pressac are mere unfounded conjectures.

All the same, even the new number of cremations adopted by Pressac is technologically impossible. He reduces the number of those allegedly cremated in the open air in 1942 from 107,000 to 50,000, and no longer in "cremation pits" but on pyres. For 1944, he does not furnish any numbers. Thus we take for valid those given in his 1989 book: 50,000. Therefore, of the 775,000 cremated, about 100,000 were cremated in the open, and the remaining 675,000 in the crematories.

The engineer R. Jakobskötter, speaking in 1941 of the Topf ovens heated with electricity in the crematory of Erfurt, states that the second oven was able to perform 3,000 cremations, while the normal duration of the refractory walls of the ovens was 2,000 cremations.[40] The Gusen oven lasted for 3,200 cremations,[41] after which it was necessary to dismantle it and replace the fire-resistant walls.[42] The duration of one chamber was therefore about 1,600 cremations. Now, even supposing that the ovens of Auschwitz-Birkenau were used to the extreme limit of 3,000 cremations per chamber, altogether they would have been able to cremate about 156,000 corpses (according to Pressac, the total number of the victims among the registered prisoners was 130,000 (p. 146)), while the cremation of 675,000 corpses would have required at least four complete substitutions of the fire-resistant walls of all the chambers. This means that for Crematories II and III alone, 256 tons of fire-resistant wall material would have been necessary (not counting that for the gasogenes), with a labor time (based on that required at Gusen) of about 7,200 hours.

All the same, in the archives of the Bauleitung that were left "intact" by the SS of Auschwitz, which Pressac has examined in their entirety, there is not a trace of these enormous projects, which means that they were never carried out, for in these records, there exists, to give an example, «un réglement de comptes administratifs acharné» ["a tenacious administrative settlement of accounts"] between the Bauleitung and Topf of even a meager payment of 828 marks (p. 59).

The cremation of 675,000 corpses is technologically impossible, and consequently no mass extermination was perpetrated at Auschwitz-Birkenau.

The extermination of Hungarian Jews

Jean-Claude Pressac, embarrassed by the technical impossibility of a mass cremation of the Hungarian Jews alleged to have been gassed, plays at reduction, declaring that of the aproximately 438,000 deportees to Auschwitz-Birkenau, 146,000 were able to work and therefore were saved; the 292,000 remaining were incapable of work, and were gassed (p. 147). He refers to the statistical estimates of G. Wellers, who represents Establishment orthodoxy on the matter, and according to whom the number of people gassed was 410,000 (p. 147).

From these, Pressac calculates that with a total capacity of Crematories II, III, and IV, and of the "cremation pits" of 3,300 corpses per day, with the possibility of an extension to 4,300 (Pressac does not say how), «les SS pouvaient anéantir en 70 jour jusqu'à 300.000 personnes» (p. 148) ["the SS could annihilate up to 300,000 people in seventy days."]

Regarding the first point, because Pressac does not furnish any proof of the transfer of (146,000 - 28,000 registered [prisoners] =) 118,000 Hungarian Jews from Auschwitz, with the same logic one can claim that (438,000 - 28,000 =) 410,000 Hungarian Jews were transferred from Auschwitz, and thus did not undergo extermination.

Regarding the second point, we notice immediately the capacity indicated by Pressac is technically impossible: Crematories II, III, and V, would have been able to cremate at the most 900 corpses, while the "cremation pits", as we have indicated, are a technical absurdity.

Nevertheless, the deportation of the Hungarian Jews took place from 15 May to 8 July 1944, in a time frame of 54 days, not 70; therefore, even assuming the maximum capacity of 4,300 corpses per day (54 x 4,300), it would have been possible to cremate 232,200 corpses, not 292,000. As a matter of fact, after eliminating the pauses between the various waves of deportation and the actual days of deportation and arrival of deportees to Auschwitz, which were 39,[43] the installations at Birkenau would have been capable of cremating 39 x 4,300 = 167,700 corpses. And where would the remaining 124,300 corpses have been put?

It is pointed out also that the aerial photographs taken by the Allied military on 31 May 1944,[44] at the crucial time of presumed extermination, on the day of the arrival at Birkenau of about 15,000 deportees, and after 14 days of intense arrivals (184,000 deportees, averaging 13,000 per day) and with an extermination toll (according to Pressac's hypothesis) of at least 110,000 homicidally gassed, which would have had to average 7,800 per day, every single day for 14 consecutive days; after all of that, the photographs do not show the slightest evidence of this alleged enormous extermination: No trace of smoke, no trace of pits, crematory or otherwise, burning or not, no sign of dirt extracted from pits, no trace of wood set aside for use in pits, no sign of vehicles or of any other type of activity in the crucial zones of the courtyard of Crematory V nor in the earth of Bunker 2, nor in Crematories II and III. These photographs[45] constitute irrefutable proof that the story of extermination of the Hungarian Jews is historically unfounded.

Chapter Four

The "Final Solution"

Jean-Claude Pressac states that the last stage of the "final solution"[46]

> ne fut decidée par les autorités SS de Berlin qu'à partir de mai-juin 1942, pour être ensuite concretisée techniquement par les SS de la Bauleitung D'Auschwitz et les ingénieurs de la firme J.A. Topf und Söhne d'Erfurt. (p. 2)

> [was not decided on by the SS authorities in Berlin until after May-June 1942, and only subsequently concretized technically by the SS of the Bauleitung of Auschwitz and the engineers of the firm J.A. Topf and Sons of Erfurt.]

Regarding this, Pressac reports:

> début juin 1942, Himmler ayant convoqué Höss à Berlin, l'informa du choix de son camp comme centre d'anéantissement massif des Juifs. Le chef des SS avait retenu Auschwitz parce que sa situation ferroviaire était favorable *et que le camp serait bientôt pourvu d'un extraordinaire crématoire pouvant incinérer 1.400 corps par jour* (épisode que Höss place faussement à l'été 1941 comme d'ailleurs Eichmann après l'avoir lu dans les écrites de ce dernier). L'action commencerait le 1er juillet et il fallait qu'a

cette date tout soit prêt pour l'exécuter. (p. 41, our italics)

[at the beginning of June 1942, Himmler summoned Höss to Berlin, and informed him of the choice of his camp as center for the massive annihilation of the Jews. The chief of the SS had chosen Auschwitz because of its favorable situation close to the railway, *and because the camp would soon be provided with an extraordinary crematory capable of cremating 1,400 bodies per day* (an episode that Höss wrongly places in the summer of 1941, which Eichmann also does after having read Höss' writings). The action would begin 1 July and everything would have to be ready to execute it by this date.]

In reality, it is Pressac who *wrongly* places in 1942 an event which, according to the chronological and logical developments of the events referred to by Höss, could only have taken place in 1941.

We summarize the following development:

[Höss] In the summer of 1941 — at the moment I am not able to cite the exact date — I was suddenly summoned to Berlin to the Reichsführer [Himmler], by his Aide.

[Himmler] The Führer has ordered the final solution of the Jewish question, and we SS must execute this order.

I chose Auschwitz, both for its optimal communications position and because the adjacent land can be easily isolated and camouflaged.

You will learn further details from Sturmbannführer Eichmann, of the RSHA, whom I will send to you shortly.

[Höss] Soon thereafter, Eichmann came to me at Auschwitz, where he revealed to me the plan of action for the various countries.

Hence, we went on to discuss the means of effecting the extermination plan. The means could only be gas

...

Eichmann promised that he would inform himself on the existence of an easily produced gas which would not require any particular installations, and that he would later inform me on the matter.

We went to inspect the area to establish the best location, and ascertained that it was the farm [the future Bunker 1] situated at the northwest corner of the future third sector of buildings, Birkenau.[*]

Eichmann then returned to Berlin, to report to him [Himmler] the content of our conversation.

At the end of November in Eichmann's office in Berlin a conference was held on the entire Jewish Section, at which I was invited to participate ...

We were not told when the action would begin, nor had Eichmann been able to find the appropriate gas.

In the autumn of 1941, by means of a secret order given to the prisoner of war camps, the Gestapo separated all the politruks, the commissars and some political officials and sent them to the closest concentration camp, to have them liquidated.

At Auschwitz small transports of these men were continuously arriving; they were then shot in the gravel pit by the buildings of the [tobacco] monopoly, or in the courtyard of Block II [Block 11].

On the occasion of one of my service trips, my substitute, Hauptsturmführer Fritzsch, on his own initiative, used gas to exterminate these prisoners of war; he filled the cells located in the basement to overflowing with Russians and, protecting himself with a gasmask, had Cyklon B [Zyklon B] infused, which provoked the immediate death of the victims.

On Eichmann's next visit, I reported to him on the use of Zyklon B, and we decided that it would be the gas used for the imminent mass slaughter.

---

[*] The future section BIII at Birkenau.

The killing of the Russian prisoners of war with Cyklon B, which I referred to above, continued, but no longer in Block II, because after the gassing, the entire building would have to be aired out for at least two days. As a result, the mortuary room of the crematory near the hospital was used, after the doors were rendered gas proof, and gas emission holes were opened in the ceiling.

I wouldn't know at what period exactly the extermination of the Jews began; probably already in September 1941, but perhaps only in January 1942.[47]

It is thus clear that the presumed summons of Höss to Berlin came *before* the first alleged homicidal gassing in the Bunker of Block 11 (and before the successive gassings in the Leichenhalle of Crematory I at Auschwitz); but because Pressac places this event *entre le cinque et la fin décembre* 1941 (p. 34), it is just as clear that the summons dates back to the summer of 1941, not to 1942.

Himmler's second motive for choosing Auschwitz does not find any verification in the "Annotations" *(Aufzeichnungen)* and in the sworn testimonies of R. Höss, but is the simple fruit of the fantasy of Jean-Claude Pressac, which is equal to imagining both the precise date of the presumed summons (at the beginning of June), as well as the date of the beginning of extermination (1 July).

One may ask why Pressac would begin his book with these manipulations. The answer is simple: Not having found any evidence in Moscow of criminal aims in the plans of the crematories of Birkenau, and being forced to admit that these crematories were initially foreseen *sans chambres à gas homicides* (without homicidal gas chambers) (p. 53), he had to postpone the alleged decision to exterminate the Jews by one year, because otherwise the planning of four crematories without gas chambers in the very place destined to be the principal center of such an extermination would have appeared too unlikely. Pressac falls into contradiction nevertheless, because he places the beginning of the homicidal activities in Bunker 1 at the end of May 1942 (p. 39), that is, before R. Höss knew or received the alleged extermination order from Himmler (beginning of June). Here, it is opportune to remember that the beginning of the activity at Bunker 1 was placed in January 1942 in the first edition of *Kalendarium of Auschwitz*;[48] in the second edition, it is moved to March.[49] Pressac finally moves it to the end of May. In all three cases this was done without any proof of any kind. In addition, because the second edition of *Kalendarium of Auschwitz* places the beginning of the activity in Bunker 2 at 30 June 1942,[50] it is evident that R. Höss theoretically must have been summoned to Berlin at the beginning of June, and it matters little that R. Höss never specifies it: Jean-Claude Pressac decrees it authoritatively.

Thus it is clear that the declaration of R. Höss on the presumed summons to Berlin by Himmler in June 1941 upsets Pressac's reasoning from the very beginning.

Granting this, let us now follow this reasoning in its successive logical and chronological development.

As indicated, Pressac places the first homicidal gassing between 5 December 1941 and the end of that month (p. 34). Regarding this, Pressac writes:

> D'après Höss (qui n'y assista pas) la mort aurait été immédiate. D'autres parlent d'un gazage ayant duré deux jours avec introduction d'une seconde quantité de toxique parce que la première n'avait pas tué tout le monde. De l'acide cyanhydrique, se vaporisant à 27°C, utilisé dans un sous-sol *non encore chauffé* en plein hiver silésien e une *méconnaissance de la dose*

létale pourraient expliquer la durée anormale de ce gazage. (p. 34, our italics)

[According to Höss (who did not take part), death would have been immediate. Others speak of a gassing having lasted two days, with the introduction of a second toxic quantity because the first did not kill everyone. Hydrocyanic acid, vaporizing at 27°C, used in an *as yet unheated* basement in full Silesian winter and a *misreading of the lethal dose* could explain the abnormal duration of this gassing.]

It is known that this presumed event was supposed to have occured, according to the *Auschwitz Kalendarium,* on the basis of various eyewitnesses, between 3 and 5 September 1941.[51] The Polish historian S. Klodzinski, with the help of responses to a questionnaire on the first alleged gassing which he sent to 250 former prisoners of Auschwitz who were registered before September 1941, alters the date of this gassing to between 5 and 9 September 1941.[52] Pressac, who in 1989 still followed the *Auschwitz Kalendarium* literally,[53] moves the date by at least three months: On what basis? On the basis of our 190-page study *Auschwitz: La Prima Gasazione,*[54] in which we show that this event has no historic foundation because it is not supported by any document, but is instead contradicted by the available documents, and finally, that all the testimonies on this subject are contradictory on all their essential points. Pressac, instead of accepting this inevitable conclusion, assumes one of our polemical observations is true,[55] then decrees that this supposed event not only has a historic reality, but *de nos jours* (at the present time) (p. 34) its official date is that which he has indicated.

Here Pressac gives one of many examples of his captious methodology. The story of the introduction of a second quantity of Zyklon B comes from the testimony of M. Kula (deposition of 11 June 1945),[56] which, however, places the first homicidal gassing with absolute certainty in August 1941:

> According to my information, the first gassing took place the night of the 14–15 and the day of the 15th of August 1941, in the Bunkers of Block 11. I remember this date exactly, because it coincides with the anniversary of my arrival at the camp, and because then the first Russian prisoners of war were gassed.[57]

M. Kula is the witness from whom Pressac takes the story of the *quattre colonnes grillagées* (four wire-latticed columns) for introducing Zyklon B in the supposed gas chambers of Crematories II and III (p. 74).[58]

Pressac's explanation for the "abnormal" duration of the supposed gassing is the cold temperature and ignorance of the lethal dose. These claims are already discredited in our book on the basis of testimony from the *same* witnesses:

(witness Glowacki: "there was a tremendous heat"; witness Kielar: the air was very "suffocating, hot").

They are also refuted by practical experiences during disinfestation of the barracks with Zyklon B during the years 1940 to 1941 at times when the local temperatures were between -4°C and -8°C, during which the gas developed to its maximum extent after one or two hours.[59] Finally, in this work we have shown that the lethal dose of hydrocyanic acid for human beings was perfectly well known since the 1930s, on the basis of *Schädliche Gase, Dämpfe, Nebel, Rauch und Staubarten* (Verlag von Julius Springer, Berlin 1931), the classic by Ferdinand Flury and Franz Zernik. This is in direct contradiction to the statements of Jean-Claude Pressac (see above).[60]

Pressac's thesis involves another contradiction, because this supposed event, predating by at least five months the decision to exterminate the Jews, evidently has no connection with this, any more than do the successive gassings in the Leichenhalle of Crematory I of Auschwitz, from January 1941. All the same, Pressac affirms that at the end of April, difficulties having arisen, it was decided *de transférer ce genre d'activité à Birkenau* (p. 35); in other words, it was decided to put into operation Bunker 1, which however was linked with the extermination of the Jews.

Here Pressac therefore ruptures the consecutive logic (i.e. logically admissible, but historically false) which he put forth in his 1989 book:

> Because the lethal dose for humans was not known, the SS had made a botched trial gassing in the basement of Bunker 11 of the Stammlager on 3, 4, and 5 September 1941, the victims being 850 Soviet POWs and other prisoners.
>
> It was subsequently seen to be more convenient to gas people as required in the very place where all corpses inevitably had to go eventually: the morgue of Krematorium I.
>
> But trials to perfect the technique could not be carried out in this crematory attached to the camp, hence the idea of establishing Bunker 1 in an isolated location on the edge of Birkenau wood.[61]

As regards the "final solution," Pressac inflicts the final blow to the traditional interpretation of the Wannsee conference declaring in this connection:

> Le 20 janvier [1942], se tenait à Berlin la conférence dite de Wannsee. Si une action de ‹refoulement› des Juifs vers l'Est fut bien prévue avec l'évocation d'une élimination ‹naturelle› par le travail, personne ne parla alors de liquidation industrielle. *Dans les jours et les semaines qui suivirent, la Bauleitung d'Auschwitz ne reçut ni appel, ni télégramme, ni lettre réclamant l'étude d'une installation adaptée à cette fin.* (p. 35, our italics)

[January 20, 1942, the so-called Wannsee conference was held in Berlin. If an operation to 'expel' the Jews towards the East was indeed anticipated with the evocation of a 'natural' elimination by work, no one spoke then of industrial liquidation. *In the days and weeks that followed, the Bauleitung of Auschwitz received neither appeal, nor telegram, nor letter calling for an installation adapted to this end.*]

The story of this supposed "final solution," begun with a *verbal* order from Himmler, could only have been concluded with another *verbal* order:

Fin novembre [1944], sur ordre verbal d'Himmler, les gazages homicides furent arrêtés. (p. 93)

[The end of November (1944), on the verbal order of Himmler, the homicidal gassings were stopped.]

Needless to say, there is no proof of the existence of this "verbal order."[62]

Chapter Five

Crematories II and III

Jean-Claude Pressac affirms that a capacity of 1,440 corpses per day was foreseen for the new crematory destined for the principal camp, which later became the prototype of Crematories II and III at Birkenau (p. 28). As we have seen, that is precisely what would have induced Himmler to choose Auschwitz for carrying out the extermination of the Jews (p. 41); nevertheless he specifies that:

> bien que le crématoire II ait servi de catalyseur pour la choix d'Auschwitz dans la liquidation des Juifs, il ne se rattache pas directement à cette extermination, mais est considéré comme un moyen supplétif occasionnel; le crématoire III n'est projeté qu'en complément du II, pour faire face à un effectif de 200,000 détenus, et n'est ‹criminalisé› que pour les besoins de la burocratie SS. (pp. 54–55)

> [Although Crematory II has served as a catalyst for the choice of Auschwitz in the liquidation of the Jews, it is not linked directly to this extermination, but is considered as an occasional supplementary means; Crematory III is planned only as an extension of II, to deal with an effective 200,000 prisoners, and is only 'criminalized' by the needs of the bureaucracy.]

Crematory III had a "sanitary orientation" (p. 50), equal to Crematory II, of which it was naturally the extension; the structures of Crematory II and III were not planned with the intention of homicidal gassing (p. 63), and none of the four crematories at Birkenau initially anticipated homicidal gas chambers (p. 53). Crematories IV and V instead "belonged to Bunkers 1 and 2" (p. 50); they were "destined to Bunkers 1 and 2" (p. 52), "connected directly to Bunkers 1 and 2" (p. 54).

So according to Pressac, Crematories II and III initially had a normal hygienic-sanitary function, while Crematories IV and V (which were not equipped with homicidal gas chambers) had a criminal function because they were supposed to have cremated alleged homicidally gassed cadavers of Bunkers 1 and 2.

This results in the meaningless conclusion that the *Auschwitz Bauleitung* technicians assigned thirty chambers (presumed capacity: 2,880 corpses per day) to the normal health measures of the camp, and only sixteen chambers to mass extermination. In other words, they expected more corpses from the natural mortality of the camp than from mass extermination!

Another Pressac conclusion, even more revealing, is that Auschwitz was chosen by Himmler to commence extermination of Jews because of the design of the new crematory, which Pressac presumes could cremate 1,440 corpses per day. The Bauleitung technicians however, instead of making this crematory and its twin Crematory III the fulcrum of the extermination, turned to two other crematories of distinctly lower capacity!

Regarding the genesis of the other three Crematories (III, IV and V), Pressac writes:

> Le 19 [août] est à considérer comme la date où fut

entérinée la décision de construire trois autres crématoires à Birkenau, dont deux étaient liés directement au processus criminel d'anéantissement des
Juifs. (p. 49)

[The 19th (August) is to be considered the date when
the decision to build three other crematories at
Birkenau was ratified, of which two were linked
directly to the criminal process of annihilation of the
Jews.]

But 19 August is also a date on which a terrible
typhus epidemic raged at Auschwitz-Birkenau that
decimated the prisoners of the camp.

Pressac himself admits that:

la pression de l'épidemie de typhus, avec chaque jour
ses 250 à 300 morts parmi les détenus, ainsi que les
civils et SS les accompagnant dans l'au-delà, con-
juguée aux incessantes arrivées de convois juifs,
poussa Bischoff, sur demande de Höss, à précipiter la
réalisation du programme crématoire et à le doubler.
(p. 50)

[the pressure of the typhus epidemic, with its 250 to
300 deaths among the prisoners each day, as well as
the civilians and SS accompanying them to the hereafter, plus the incessant arrivals of Jewish convoys,
pushed Bischoff, on Höss' orders, to expedite the crematory program.]

Actually, the decision to construct four crematories at
Birkenau depended exclusively on the terror which
the typhus epidemic provoked in the SS,[63] in light of
the proposed expansion of the camp's population by
about ten times.

Pressac shows that the installations and the precau-
tions of the SS, which were aimed at halting the
typhus epidemic, bore the designation *special*
(Sonder) in the SS terminology.

Doctor Wirths:

> prévoyait un retour du typhus si des ‹mesures spé-
> ciales› *(Sondermassnahmen)* pour améliorer la situa-
> tion sanitaire n'étaient pas prises d'urgence. (p. 82,
> our italics)

> [foresaw a return of the typhus if some 'special mea-
> sures' *(Sondermassnahmen)* to improve the sanitary
> situation were not taken urgently.]

Pressac explains correctly that:

> les termes ‹mesures spéciales/ Sondermassnahmen›
> et ‹mesures de construction spéciales/Sonderbau-
> massnahmen› désignent des dispositions liées aux
> questions sanitaires ou aux bâtiments s'y rapportant
> (par exemple, alimentation en eau, *mesures d'hygiène
> appliquées aux détenus,* etc. (p. 107, note 256, our
> italics)

> [the terms 'special measures/Sondermassnahmen'
> and 'special measures of construction/Sonderbau-
> massnahmen' designate the dispositions relating to
> the sanitary issues or to the buildings if involved (for
> example, water supply, *hygienic measures applied to
> the prisoners,* etc.]

With the construction of the disinfection and disinfestation installation of the Zentralsauna:

> les SS voulaient contrer ‹définitivement› toute résur-
> gence du typhus à Birkenau. (p. 69)

> [the SS wanted to 'definitively' counter any resur-
> gence of the typhus at Birkenau.]

Now the *Zentralsauna* was in fact part of the *Sonderbaumassnahmen* (p. 107, note 256) and, as with the
crematories, was involved in the *Durchführung der
Sonderbehandlung* (implementation of such special
measures) (p. 61).

If, therefore, the construction of the new crematory
had a purely sanitary purpose (by Pressac's admis-
sion), it should have been undertaken immediately
«en raison de la situation crée par les ‹actions spé-

ciales› », as is stated in a document of the end of July 1942 (p. 47), a time of full typhus epidemic; it is clear that these "special actions" *(Sonderaktionen)* were linked to the fight against the epidemic and had no criminal connotation.

And, if the same document mentions «4 Stück Baracken für Sonderbehandlung *der Häftlinge* in Birkenau» (p. 46, our italics) ["4 barracks for the special treatment *of prisoners* at Birkenau"], it is equally clear that even this "special treatment," reserved for the registered *prisoners* of the camp, referred simply to the «mesures d'hygiène appliquées aux détenus» ["sanitary measures put into practice for the prisoners"], to use the words of Jean-Claude Pressac.

And, if finally on 26 August 1942, during a full typhus epidemic, Zyklon B was picked up at Dessau *für Sonderbehandlung,* it is still clear that it served disinfestation purposes (p. 47).[*]

Self-contradictingly, Pressac instead claims that the *Sonderbehandlung* was a convenient term that designated «la liquidation par le gaz des inaptes juifs à Birkenau» (p. 46) ["the liquidation by gas of the unfit

---

[*] In the Auschwitz construction plan of 28 October 1942, a disinfestation facility *Entwesungsanlage* of 1,000m² *für Sonderbehandlung* was foreseen and planned specifically for the hygienic-sanitary treatment of the prisoners; it was endowed with heat, showers, and disinfestation installations *(Heiz-Brause- u. Desinfektionsanlage)* and had a cost of 73,680 RM. Another *Entwesungsanlage* smaller (262.84m²) was destined for the guard troops *(für die Wachtruppe). Zusammenstellung des Bauvorhaben Kriegsgefangenenlager Auschwitz (Durchführung der Sonderbehandlung, 28 Oktober 1942.* Photocopy in: *Florian Freund, Bertrand Perz, Karl Stuhlpfaffer, Der Bau des Vernichtungslager Auschwitz-Birkenau. Zeitgeschichte, Heft 5/6, Mai-Juni 1993, p. 207).*

Jews at Birkenau."] He further specifies that:

> l'acte de mise à mort en lui-même était dit ‹traitement spécial› ou ‹transfert de population juive› alors que la globalité de l'opération, incluant sélection, transport des inaptes et gazage homicide, s'énonçait ‹action spécial›, terme n'étant pourtant pas spécifiquement criminel car pouvant s'appliquer à une opération qui ne l'était pas. (p. 46)

> [the act of putting to death itself, was called 'special treatment' or 'transfer of Jewish population,' because the totality of the operation, including selection, transfer of the unfit and homicidal gassing, was termed 'special action,' a term not specifically criminal, because it could apply to an operation that was not.]

Pressac himself mentions a case in which the term *Sonderaktion* had no criminal meaning; after the *strike* (in an extermination camp!) of the civilian workers on 17 and 18 December 1942, the Gestapo made a *Sonderaktion* consisting of the interrogation of the workers to find out what had produced the refusal to work (p. 63).

Neither *Sondermassnahmen*, nor *Sonderbaumassnahmen*, nor *Sonderbehandlung*, nor *Sonderaktion* had a criminal significance and Jean-Claude Pressac does not introduce a single document to support the contrary. Therefore, his deductions have no foundation.

What Pressac writes about the supply of Zyklon B to Auschwitz is really a bit incredible. He pretends that the SS-WVHA knew nothing about the typhus epidemic that raged at Auschwitz-Birkenau in 1942. This epidemic required enormous quantities of Zyklon B for the purpose of disinfestation. He maintains that the administration of the camp, which did not want the WVHA to know of the epidemic, could not request

Zyklon B without betraying itself. This is how he extricates himself:

> Une astuce fut trouvée. Mettre sur le dos des Juifs les effarantes quantités de gaz employées. L'autorisation de transport accordée le 26 août le fut pour ‹traitement spécial›. Bien que les responsables du SS-WVHA de Berlin sussent la finalité du ‹traitement›, ils en ignoraient les modalités, c'est-à-dire les quantités de toxique utilisées. Ce qui permit de leur faire croire que la majorité du Zyklon-B livré servait aux gazage homicides dans les Bunker 1 et 2, alors que 2 à 3% suffisait. Ainsi, 97 à 98% du gaz pouvait être consacré à l'épouillage. (p. 47)

> [A ruse was devised. The blame for the bewildering quantities of gas used was placed on the Jews. The shipment authorization given on 26 August was for 'special treatment.' Although the authorities of the SS-WVHA[*] of Berlin knew the end result of the 'treatment,' they were unaware of the specifics, that is, the quantities of toxin used. Because 2% to 3% was enough, this allowed them to make others think that the majority of the Zyklon B delivered was needed for homicidal gassings in Bunker 1 and 2. In this manner, 97% to 98% of the gas could be used for delousing.]

The goal of this reasoning is quite clear: Because the reason for the ordering Zyklon B are apparently two-fold — on the one hand the "special treatment" (*Sonderbehandlung*: procurement of 26 August) and the "resettlement of Jews" (*Judenumsiedlung*: 2 October), terms that Pressac interprets in the criminal sense; on the other hand, the disinfestation (*Gas zur Desinfektion des Lagers* [gas for disinfesting of the camp]: 29 July)[64] — there would exist two types of procurements, bureaucratically defined: one for gassing Jews, the other for disinfestation of the camp.

---

[*] SS-WVHA = (Wirtschafts-Verwaltungshauptamt: Economic and Administrative Offices of the SS)

But in this case, the quantity of Zyklon B for a homicidal purpose would be enormous (the request of 2 October alone refers to 5 tons gross), in contradiction to the thesis advanced by Pressac in his 1989 book, that only 2–3 percent of the Zyklon B supplied to Auschwitz was used for the purpose of homicide.[65] To overcome this contradiction, Pressac has found nothing better than to assert that the request for Zyklon B, supposedly for the purpose of homicide (*Sonderbehandlung, Judenumsiedlung*), was in reality only a camouflage for a request with a sanitary purpose! Just how far the WVHA was unaware of the epidemic of typhus that raged at Auschwitz can be deduced from the fact that Doctor Wirths, who on 6 September 1942 had been:

> nommé médicin-chef de la garrison du camp d'Auschwitz afin d'enrayer l'épidémie de typhus, (p. 116)

> [named chief doctor of the garrison of the camp at Auschwitz in order to retard the epidemic of typhus]

came from the Inspectorate of the Concentration Camps,[66] that is, from the Amtsgruppe D of the WVHA.

Realizing the naivete of his reasoning, Pressac seeks to render the picture he has drawn more credible by fabricating the purpose of Pohl's visit of 23 September 1942 to Auschwitz:

> Le chef du SS-WVHA, le géneral de corps d'armée SS Pohl, se présenta à l'improviste dans la matinée du 23 septembre 1942 à Auschwitz *pour savoir ce qui s'y passait et où filaient les tonnes de Zyklon-B accordées.* Pohl se rendit d'abord à la Bauleitung, se fit expliquer l'implantation générale du camp, décrire les batiments achevés, en cours (dont les quatre crématoires de Birkenau) et en projet. *A sa question sur le Zyklon-B, il lui fut répondu qu'avec ce produit, on*

49

détruisait à la fois les poux et les Juifs. (p. 59, **our** italics)

[The Chief of the SS-WVHA, General of the SS Army Corps Pohl, presented himself unexpectedly in the morning of the 23rd of September at Auschwitz *to learn what was going on, and where the assigned tons of Zyklon B were going.* Pohl went first to the Bauleitung, and had the general set-up of the camp explained to him, and the buildings that had been erected, those under construction (including the four crematories of Birkenau) and those planned described to him. *His question on Zyklon B was answered that with this product the Jews and the lice were destroyed at the same time.*]

Pressac's source for the above is the diary of Johann Paul Kremer published in *Auschwitz vu par le SS* (Edition du Musée d'Etat à Oswiecim) [*Auschwitz Viewed by the SS* (Edition of the State Museum at Oswiecim, 1974)], pages 233 and 234 (notes 182 and 183 on p. 105). In reality, these two pages from the end of page 233 to the end of page 234, read as follows:

La matin, l'Obergruppenführer Pohl est arrivée avec sa suite au Foyer des Waffen SS. Devant la porte, une sentinelle. Pour la première fois, on me présente les armes. Le soir, à 20 heures, dîner au Foyer des officiers SS en compagnie de l'Obergruppenführer Pohl: un véritable festin. On nous a servi du brochet frit à volonté, du vrai café, une excellente bière et des sandwiches.

[In the morning, Obergruppenführer Pohl arrived with his entourage, at the residence of the Waffen SS. In front of the door a sentinel. For the first time I am presented arms. The evening at 20 hours; dinner at the SS Officers Club in the company of Obergruppenführer Pohl: a real feast. We were served fried pike all we wanted, real coffee, an excellent beer and some sandwiches.]

That is all. The rest is the product of Pressac's imagination. On p. 117 he twice contradicts himself, by writing that Pohl had gone to Auschwitz:

> surtout préoccupé de construire une grande station
> d'épuration des eaux à Broschkowitz (au nord de la
> ville d'Auschwitz) *pour réduire le risque typhoïdique.*
> (p. 117, our italics)

> [above all, concerned with constructing a large water
> purification station at Broschkowitz (north of the
> town of Auschwitz) *to reduce the risk of typhus.*]

Therefore, the WVHA already knew of the typhus epidemic and Pohl did not inspect Auschwitz to ask «où filaient les tonnes de Zyklon-B accordées» ["where the tons of Zyklon B given them were going."]

Jean-Claude Pressac's fundamental thesis is that Crematories II and III, planned and constructed as simple sanitary installations, were successively turned into instruments of crime:

> S'imposa fin octobre 1942 l'idée, somme toute évidente, de transférer l'activité ‹gazeuse› des Bunker 1 et 2 dans une pièce de crématoire, équipée d'une ventilation artificielle, comme cela avait été pratiqué en décembre 1941 dans la morgue du crématoire I. (p. 60)

> [Towards the end of October 1942, the idea occured, an obvious one when all was said and done, of transferring the 'gassing' activity of Bunkers 1 and 2 into a room of the crematory, equipped with artificial ventilation, as had been practiced in 1941 in the morgue of Crematory I.]

That is an arbitrary statement by Pressac, not supported by any document. He adds an equally unfounded assertion, that:

> en novembre 1942, les SS de la Bauleitung résolurent d'équiper les crématoires de chambres à gaz homicides. (p. 66)

> [In November 1942, the SS of the Bauleitung resolved to equip the crematories with homicidal gas

chambers.]

According to Pressac, initially the intentions of the SS were to:

> utiliser pour les gazages la ‹Leichenkeller 1› du cré- matoire II dès qu'elle serait opérationelle ou, si l'expédition des matériels requis tardait, se rabattre sur la ‹Leichenhalle› du crématoire I aprés avoir installé sa désaération définitive, déjà livrée, et capa- ble d'extraire 8.300 m³ d'air par heure de toutes les pièces du bâtiment, dont environ 3.000 m³ par heure de sa ‹Leichenhalle.› (p. 61)

> [use the 'Leichenkeller 1' of Crematory II for the gas- sings as soon as it was operational. Or, if shipment of the required material was delayed, to fall back on the 'Leichenhalle' of Crematory I after having installed its final ventilators, already delivered. These ventila- tors were capable of extracting 8,300 m³ of air per hour from all the rooms of the building, and about 3,000 m³ per hour from its 'Leichenhalle.']

This appears clearly irrational, even from Pressac's perspective. Granted, on the one hand, that the Baule- itung could have continued to use Bunkers 1 and 2 as it had done until then for mass extermination of the Jews while they were waiting for the requested mate- rials to arrive for the homicidal transformation of Leichenkeller 1 of Crematory II; but on the other hand, the gassings had already been transferred to the end of April 1942 from Crematory I at Birkenau because:

> un gazage imposait d'isoler totalement la zone du crématoire, ce qui perturbait l'activité du camp,

> [gassing demanded total isolation of the crematory zone, which disturbed the activity of the camp],

and in addition:

> il était impraticable lorsque les travaux étaient en cours, (p. 35)

[it was impracticable, while work was in progress],
(which occurred fairly often.)

The idea that the SS were thinking again of moving
the supposed homicidal gassings to Crematory I
occurs to Pressac because a note dated 27 November
1942 gives the order to install the ventilation system
of Crematory I (p. 60). Nevertheless, he states at the
same time that:

> sa morgue étant désaérée mécaniquement, des gaza-
> ges homicides avec un toxique gazeux pouvaient y
> être pratiqués. (p. 23)

> [homicidal gassings with a toxic agent could be car-
> ried out there because its morgue was mechanically
> ventilated.]

(Referring to the temporary ventilation system
mounted in Crematory I by the Boos company
between 23 February and 1 March 1941 [p. 18].)

Therefore, if the temporary ventilation system could
already support the homicidal gassings, why install a
permanent system? If instead the permanent system
was indispensable for homicidal gassings, why wasn't
it installed immediately instead of being left in a storage room? It had been shipped from Topf 16 April
1942. Then the idea to use Crematory I for mass gassings was discarded, and the Bauleitung concentrated
on the criminal transformation of Crematory II and
III:

> Transférer les gazages homicides dans les créma-
> toires II et III semblait simple sur le papier, mais
> l'était beaucoup moins du fait que le bâtiment, conçu
> par Prüfer et amélioré par Werkmann, n'avait pas
> été envisage à cette fin. *Le rez-de-chaussée,* avec la
> salle des fours et ses pièces de service, *n'avait besoin
> d'être modifié.* Mais le sous-sol devait etre amenagé
> pour que puissent s'y pratiquer les ‹actions spéciales›.
> (pp. 63–64, our italics)

[Transference of the homicidal gassings to Crematories II and III seemed easy on paper, but was much
less so because of the fact that the building, planned
by Prüfer and improved by Werkmann, had not been
envisioned for this purpose. *The ground floor,* with its
oven room and service rooms, *did not need to be modified.* But the basement had to be arranged so that
the 'special actions' could be carried out there.]

There is no doubt that beginning with the end of 1942,
the basement of Crematory II had undergone various
transformations with respect to the initial project.
There is also no doubt that the oven room had not
undergone any modification in number or capacity
with respect to the initial plan. How to explain this
inconsistency? If Crematory II had been planned as a
simple sanitary installation, adequate for the natural
death toll of the camp, its transformation into an
instrument of mass extermination would have
required a corresponding increase in the capacity of
the ovens: in other words, the installation of addi-
tional ovens. But that did not happen. Therefore, all
that remains is to inflate excessively the real capacity
of the ovens and, contradictingly, to infer that the
ovens could handle even a mass extermination without difficulty even though they were designed for
hygienic purposes. It suffices to declare that Crematory II could *really* cremate 1,440 corpses in 24 hours
(capacity that could be defined as technically prepos-
terous) to overcome the contradiction.

The reality is quite different. The installation in Crematory II and III of a 210 m^2 gas chamber (the area of
Leichenkeller 1), in which it would have been possible
to gas 1,800 victims without difficulty (the eyewitnesses speak even of 3,000), would have required 75
chambers instead of the existing 15 for the cremation
of the corpses in one day. The time required to cremate the bodies of the victims, would have taken five

days, presenting a serious obstacle to an extermination process. The fact, therefore, that the oven room was *not* transformed, demonstrates that the changes made in the basement were not of a criminal nature.

The picture of the changes made in the basements of Crematories II and III once more relies on Plan 2003 of 19 December 1942, which Pressac considers a *bavure architecturale** (an architectural trace), in which the slide *(Rutsche)* for the corpses no longer appears:

> l'escalier nord devient le seul accès possible aux morgues, ce qui implique que les morts devront descendre l'escalier en marchant. (pp. 64–65)

> [The north stairway becomes the only possible access to the morgues, which implies that the dead will have to descend the stairs walking.]

Actually, Plan 2003 was nothing more than a proposal to transfer the basement access to the street side *(Verlegung des Kellerzuganges an die Strassenseite)*[67] and not a plan to eliminate the slide. Therefore, the absence of the slide is basically a simplification of a part of the design which is technically irrelevant. The elimination of the slide would have been technically irrational (unless the lift were used to transport the corpses to the mortuary rooms), because the natural mortality at the camp continued. In fact, the slide was

---

* With the term *bavure* Pressac means:

> «toute indication relevée dans un document quelconque (écrit, plan, photo) relatif à un emploi anormal des crématoires et ne pouvant s'expliquer que par le gazage massif d'êtres humains» (p. 60)

> [Any indication noted in any document whatsoever (writing, plan, photo) relating to an abnormal use of the crematories that could only be explained by the massive gassing of human beings.]

constructed according to the original design both in Crematory II and in Crematory III. This was independent of the fact that:

le plan 2003 arriva trop tard sur les chantiers 30 [Crematory II] and 30a [Crematory III] (p. 65)

[Plan 2003 arrived too late at construction site 30 (Crematory II) and 30a (Crematory III)],

as Pressac claims. That, however, could not be valid for Crematory III (which was in a less advanced construction stage) but, more precisely, depended on the logical necessity of an easy access for the corpses to the mortuary chambers.

The initial plan of the SS (November 1942) was to install in Crematories II and III two homicidal gas chambers operating alternately:

Les SS envisagèrent aussi que les deux morgues fussent utilisées en chambres à gaz, croyant alors à tort que le fort rendement prévu des cinq fours trimoufle permettrait une marche alternative. Dans cette configuration, un vestiaire extérieur était indispensable, donnant directement sur l'escalier de service, qui desservait les deux salles par le vestibule central. De plus, améliorer la ventilation de la Leichenkeller 2 (seulement desaérée) s'imposait, par adjoncton d'une aeration. *Apres que les fours eurent été testés et leur rendement mieux estimé,* cette solution fut rejetée parce qu'elle aboutissait à produire au sous-sol des monceaux de cadavres que les fours du rez-de-chaussée auraient mis trop longtemps a incinérer. (p. 66, our italics)

[The SS had also envisioned that the two morgues be used as gas chambers, at that time wrongly believing that the large yield foreseen for the five three-chambered ovens would permit an alternative operation. In this configuration, an exterior changing room was indispensable, opening directly on the service stairs that connected the two rooms through the central vestibule. Moreover, it was further essential to

improve the ventilation of Leichenkeller 2 by the
addition of blower type ventilation. At the time it was
only ventilated by aspiration, that is, by drawing air
out of the room. *After the ovens had been tested and
their yield better estimated,* this solution was rejected
because it ended up producing a heap of corpses in
the basement which the ovens on the ground floor
would have taken too long to incinerate.]

Here Pressac ensnares himself in another series of
insuperable contradictions. On one hand, the plan of
the dualistic homicidal gas chamber, which depended
on an overestimate of the capacity of the ovens, could
not have been done in November 1942, because the
two three-chambered ovens of the crematory of
Buchenwald — that were of the same model as the
ovens in Crematories II and III of Birkenau — went
into operation on 23 August and on 3 October 1942
respectively (p. 39). In November therefore, the oven's
real capacity was perfectly known, having already
been in activity a total of four months. Furthermore,
the plan of the dualistic homicidal gas chamber could
not have been abandoned in November 1942 in consequence of the real capacity resulting from the testing
of the ovens, because the *first* test of the ovens in Crematory II took place, according to Pressac, on 4 March
1943 (p. 72).

What remains sure is that Jean-Claude Pressac
admits the irrationality of a plan which envisioned, in
the basement of the crematories, a capacity of corpses
enormously greater than that of the ovens on the
ground floor. In fact, he even states that these gas
chambers were divided in two to balance the process
of extermination. The capacity of the ovens being (in
his opinion, lacking in any technical foundation) still
inferior to that of the gas chambers:

La recherche d'un meilleur agencement se poursuivit
même après la mise en exploitation. Ainsi, fin 1943,

afin de ‹régulariser› la marche des crématoires II et III, l'administration du KL fit deviser *leurs chambres* a gaz en deux, ne consacrant plus que 100 m² au gazage, pour tuer et incinérer 500 à 700 arrivants inaptes (comprenant beaucoup d'enfants) en vingt-quatre heurs. (p. 67, our italics)

[The search for a better arrangement continued even after the start of the operation. Thus, at the end of 1943, so as to 'standardize' the running of Crematories II and III, the administration of the KL had *their gas chambers* divided in two, devoting no more than 100 m² for gassing, to kill and incinerate 500 to 700 unfit arrivals (including many children) in twenty-four hours.]

The source of this information is the deposition of H. Tauber, which however speaks only of Crematory II. Therefore, Pressac's attribution of this supposed modification to Crematory III, as well, is unwarranted. In his book of 1989, Pressac comments regarding H. Tauber's story concerning the division of the gas chamber and of the successive gassings as follows:

"One of the very few contestable points in the deposition."[68]

Needless to say that there is no proof of this supposed division, either documentary or architectural.

It is evident that because the maximum real capacity of Crematories II and III of 360 corpses per day (considering the presence of the corpses of children), Pressac admits *a fortiori* the pointlessness of a supposed extermination plan by the Bauleitung.

The final project of the SS, effectively accomplished, according to Pressac, was the transformation of Leichenkeller 1 into a homicidal gas chamber, and of Leichenkeller 2 into a changing room. That would mean that Crematories II and III were no longer provided with mortuary rooms. So, one may ask, where did the SS expect to deposit the corpses of the registered prisoners deceased of natural causes which had to be cremated? The question is even more legitimate in that for each of the planned Crematories II and III, we remember that originally there were envisioned three mortuary rooms, exclusively for sanitary purposes, for a total area of 671 m^2.[69]

In support of his thesis, Pressac quotes a series of *bavures* (traces) which we shall deal with subsequently. Nevertheless, the "definitive" proof is connected to the ventilation system of the crematories.

Ventilation System

The initial ventilation project of the new crematory included:

- A blowing ventilator (No.450) for the *B-Keller* (the future Leichenkeller 1) with a capacity of 4,800 m^3/h;

- An aspirating ventilator (drawing air out) (No.450) for the *B-Keller* with a capacity of 4,800 m^3/h;

- An aspirating ventilator (No.550) for the *L-Keller* (the future Leichenkeller 2) with a capacity of 10,000 m^3/h;

- An aspirating ventilator (No.550) for the oven room with a capacity of 10,000 m^3/h;

- An aspirating ventilator (No.375) with a capacity of 3,000 m^3/h for the autopsy room (p. 30).

Because Pressac indicates even the volume of the respective rooms (p. 30), it is possible to calculate the number of air exchanges estimated within one hour:

- 4,000 ÷ 483 = 9.93 exchanges for the *B-Keller*;

- 10,000 + 966 = 10.35 exchanges for the *L-Keller*;

- 10,000 + 1,031 = 9.69 exchanges for the oven room;

- 3,000 + 300 = 10 exchanges for the autopsy room.

Subsequently, the capacity of the ventilators was increased as follows:

- pumping ventilator for the *B-Keller*: 8,000 m³/h (=16.56 air exchanges per hour);

- aspirating ventilator for the *B-Keller*: 8,000 m³/h (= 16.56 air exchanges per hour);

- aspirating ventilator for the *L-Keller* 13,000 m³/h (=13.45 air exchanges per hour);

- aspirating ventilator for the oven room: 12,000 m³/h (= 11.64 air exchanges per hour)

- aspirating ventilator for the autopsy room: 4,000 m³/h (= 13.33 air exchanges per hour) (p. 38).

The capacity of the ventilators mentioned by Pressac is not certified by any document. He obviously calculated them on the basis of the power of the motors. These are shown in the D 59366 Topf plan of 10 March 1942 (Pressac's Documents 13–15) which, by its date, refers to a period in which the crematory was being planned exclusively for hygienic purposes.

Pressac states that Leichenkeller 1 of Crematories II *and* III was actually equipped with ventilators with a capacity of 8,000 m³/h of air (p. 74 and 118), and even mentions the invoice of the ventilation system for Crematory III: invoice No.729 of 27 March 1943 (p. 105, note 184).

He leaves understood that the increased capacity of the ventilators from 4,800 to 8,000 m³/h was effected to compensate for the arrangement of the ventilation system planned and built for a normal mortuary room. In fact he states, in relation to the *Gasprüfer*, which we will deal with later, that:

> les SS voulaient vérifier si la puissance de ventilation de la Leichenkeller 1 compenserait sa disposition d'origine, aération haute et désaération basse prévues pour une morgue, et qui aurait dû être inversée pour une chambre à gas, requérant aération basse et désaération haute. (pp. 71–72)

> [The SS wanted to verify if the power of the ventilation of Leichenkeller 1 would compensate for its original disposition, that is, high ventilation and low air aspiration which was anticipated for a mortuary, whereas the intention was to convert it to a gas chamber, requiring low ventilation and high air aspiration.]

Finally, by this time Leichenkeller 2, having become a changing room, no longer required a ventilation system; the ventilation systems were installed in Crematories II and III but the ventilators' motors were not. (pp. 79,80)

The study of the ventilation systems of Crematories II and III actually provides definite proof that Leichenkeller 1 was *not* transformed into a homicidal gas chamber. First of all, the Topf invoice No. 729 dated 27 March 1943[70] cited by Pressac mentions that a ventilator with a capacity of 4,800 m^3/h was required for the *B-Raum*, the supposed homicidal gas chamber, and that a ventilator with a capacity of 10,000 m^3/h was needed for the *L-Raum*, the supposed changing room. The same capacities are indicated by the invoice No. 171 of 22 February 1943 for Crematory II.[71]

In his preceding 1989 work, Pressac publishes a table which summarizes "Dimensions and volumes of the Krematorium II and III Leichenkeller" on the basis of the plans of the crematories: Leichenkeller 1 measured 30 m in length, 7 in width and 2.41 in height; therefore, it had an area of 210 m^2 and a volume of 506 m^3. Leichenkeller 2 was 49.49 m long and 7.93 m wide and 2.30 m high, so its area was 392.5 m^2, its volume was 902.7 m^3.[72] Consequently, for the supposed homicidal gas chamber, the SS had foreseen 4,800 ÷ 506 = 9.48 air exchanges per hour, while in the supposed changing room 10,000 ÷ 902.7 = 11 air exchanges per hour: thus the gas chamber was less ventilated than the changing room! But that's not all. In Engineer W. Heepke's classic work on the planning of the crematories, one reads that for the mortuary rooms it was necessary to provide a minimum of five air changes per hour, and in case of intense utilization, up to ten exchanges.[73] It is therefore evident that the ventilation system of Leichenkeller 1 was planned and built for a mortuary. As a means of comparison, seventy-two air exchanges per hour were foreseen[74] for the disinfestation gas chambers with the *Kreislauf system*, the plans of which Pressac publishes in documents 16 and 17. Additionally, we notice that seventeen air exchanges per hour were foreseen for the first ventilation plan from Topf for Crematory I of Auschwitz (p. 18). This was almost twice that of the alleged homicidal gas chamber of Crematories II and III! These plans were for the autopsy and mortuary room, without any homicidal purposes, with a purely hygienic goal.

Concerning the ventilation of Leichenkeller 2, it is true that the motor destined for this area does not figure in Plan 2197 of 19 March 1943, but that does not mean that it was decided not to install it at all. The work done in the crematories demonstrate the contrary. In Crematory II, the ventilation system of the alleged homicidal gas chamber in Leichenkeller 1 was installed between 22 February and 14 April 1943; the ventilation system of Leichenkeller 2's supposed changing room was installed between 15 and 28 March; the ventilation system of Leichenkeller 2 of Crematory III was installed between 12 and 22 April, as Pressac informs us in his 1989 book.[75] Now, if the absence of ventilator motors had been based on the SS decision to convert Leichenkeller 2 into a homicidal gas chamber, it is difficult to understand why they had the ventilation systems installed in the two crematories of Leichenkeller 2 *after* they had decided that Leichenkeller 2 did not need a ventilation system! It is therefore evident that the SS had the ventilation system of Leichenkeller 2 installed because they intended to use it. That the motors were not installed immediately was solely coincidental.

What has been presented here is already more than sufficient to cancel the criminal character of the *bavures* (traces) listed by Jean-Claude Pressac, which are in fact framed in a completely different context.

Pressac correctly states that the struggle against typhus at Auschwitz was aided by the disinfestation systems (p. 84). Since the appearance of the first cases of typhus, the SS had begun to think of expanding the existing systems; even with the introduction of new technologies (meeting of 30 June 1942) (p. 83). The compelling necessity of new disinfestation systems is confirmed by the design of the *Zentralsauna* (24 November 1942),[76] which, by its purpose of fighting the typhus epidemic, was part of the *Sonderbaumassnahmen* and came under the *Durchführung der Sonderbehandlung*. All this leads us to recall that in the meantime, at the end of 1942, the SS had decided to install several temporary disinfestation gas chambers. The first of these were in Crematories II and IV,* which were in a more advanced phase of construction.

That explains in a historical and logical manner all the *bavures* mentioned by Pressac, from which we shall take a brief respite.

- The term *Sonderkeller* applied to Leichenkeller 1 (p. 60) enters into the terminology. *Sonder-* applied to the fight against typhus.

- The term *Vergasungskeller* designates a disinfestation basement. In the explanatory report on the construction of KGL Birkenau dated 30 October 1941, the two Zyklon B *Entlausungsbaracken* (disinfestation installations) subsequently built, BW5a and 5b are equipped with a *Vergasungsraum.*[77]

- The plan to preheat Leichenkeller 1 (p. 73) makes sense for a disinfestation gas chamber because it would permit shorter gassing times (the duration of a gassing using 20g of hydrocyanic acid per square meter required 45 minutes at a temperature of 25°C to 35°C, but three hours at a temperature of 0 to 5°C).[78] It would be much less for a homicidal gas chamber, for a mass extermination in which the bodies of the victims would heat up the area sufficiently; therefore a preheating would be absolutely superfluous.[*]

---

[*] That is not unusual. Disinfestation installations were planned in the crematories at Majdanek (a), Dachau (b) and Struthof (c)

    a. Plan of 23 October 1941 (Archiwum Panstwowego Muzeum na Majdanku, sygn. VI-9a, vol.1)

    b. Plans of the «Baracke X» (crematorium) of March 1942 (No. 3884, 3885, 3887)

    c. Plan of the crematorium of 29 May 1945 (Pressac, *Technique and Operation of the Gas Chambers,* p. 561)

The presence of a gas-proof door (p. 80) is perfectly normal in a disinfestation gas chamber.

- The request for *10 Gasprüfer* (p. 71) (see appendix, Documents Nos. 7 & 8), supposing that it really deals with *Anzeigegeräte für Blausäure Reste* (implements for the indication of residues of hydrocyanic acid) (p. 72), is perfectly normal for a disinfestation gas chamber.

Instead, Pressac writes, as enthusiastically as naively:

> Ce document constitue la preuve définitive de l'existence d'une chambre à gaz *homicide* dans le crématoire II. (p. 72, our italics)

> [This document constitutes the definitive proof of the existence of a *homicidal* gas chamber in Crematory II.]

This document can be at best an *indication,* not a *definitive proof,* of the existence of a gas chamber. That this gas chamber was homicidal, however, is a simple arbitrary affirmation by Jean-Claude Pressac.

On this subject Pressac adds a very important explanation:

> Des essais avec introduction préalable de Zyklon-B furent pratiqués. La mesure du gaz cyanhydrique résiduel aurait été effectuée *par une methode chimique, et non avec les dix détecteurs de gaz,*

---

* The body of a normal adult, standing, produces 1.72 Kcal per minute [F. Flury, F. Zernik, *Schädliche Gase, Dämpfe, Nebel, Rauch und Staubarten,* Verlag von Julius Springer, Berlin 1931, p. 29]. 1,800 bodies produce therefore 3,096 Kcal per minute. The heat of vaporization of hydrocyanic acid is 6.67 Kcal/mole; because its molecular weight is 27.03, the vaporization heat of 6 kg of hydrocyanic acid is (6,000 x 6.67): 27.03 = 1,480 Kcal, less than half of the heat produced by 1,800 bodies in one minute.

demandés trop tardivement pour être livrés à temps. (p. 73, our italics)

[Some experiments with the preliminary introduction of Zyklon B were made. The measurement of the residual hydrocyanic gas would have been done *by a chemical method, and not with the ten gas detectors* requested too late to be delivered in time.]

Although this document jibes perfectly with our thesis, in our opinion, it is a forgery; of proper design, but poorly executed. To break it down:

1. The *Gasprüfer*, in the German technical terminology,[79] were simple analyzers of the combustion gases.

2. To prove the existence of hydrocyanic acid gas residue, there was only one chemical method, and no *détecteurs* (detectors) based on physical properties.[80]

3. The apparatus that was used for this test was called *Gasrestnachweisgerät für Zyklon*.[81]

4. This apparatus was required equipment at all of the disinfestation installations, including those at Auschwitz.

5. Because these devices were available in the disinfestation installations at the camp, it would not have made sense to request them from a company that did not produce them. They could have been obtained from the above-mentioned installations or ordered directly from the companies which made or distributed them (the same ones that distributed the Zyklon B).

6. Because the crematory administrations did not even request gas masks with the special filter "J" (for hydrocyanic acid), as with the *Gasprüfer*, it is clear that it was possible to procure them at the

camp, where it could also procure the *Gasrest-nachweisgeräte für Zyklon.*

Our conclusion: the *Gasprüfer* were simple analyzers of the combustion gases of the crematory ovens.

• Regarding the presence of 14 showers in Leichen-keller 1: According to Pressac, this is a *bavure* because these showers were false (p. 80), and were used therefore to deceive victims of alleged homicidal gas chambers; that these showers were *false* is a simple arbitrary statement by Pressac.

• The mention of "a wooden blower" *(Holzgebläse)* destined for Leichenkeller 1 (p. 70) is for Pressac a *bavure technique* (technical trace) because:

> prouvait que l'air extrait n'était plus celui d'une morgue, chargé de miasmes, mais de l'air mélangé à un produit aggressif ne devant être aspiré que par une soufflerie ne pouvant être corrodée, donc entière-ment de bois (de préférence en cyprès). Le toxique gazeux utilisé dans les chambres à gaz homicides était de l'acide cyanhydrique à forte concentration (20 *gr/m³*) et les acides sont corrosifs. (pp. 70–71, our italics)

> [it proved that the air extracted was no longer that of a morgue, permeated by miasmas, but air mixed with a corrosive substance which could be vented only by a non-corrodible fan, made entirely of wood (preferably cypress). The gaseous toxin used in the homicidal gas chambers was concentrated hydrocyanic acid (20 gr/m³) and the acids are corrosive.]

Nevertheless the above-mentioned wooden blower was later replaced with a metal one, as is clear from the *Aktenvermerk* of 25 March 1943,[82] which reads:

> Anstelle des Holzgebläses für die Entlüftungsanlage des *Leichenkellers I* wird ein Schmiedeeisengebläse als Ausführung gewählt.

[instead of the wooden blower for the exhaust system
of *Leichenkeller I,* a wrought-iron-type blower was
adopted into the final design].

Pressac must therefore explain why, given that
hydrocyanic acid (as he says) is corrosive, the
engineers of the Bauleitung replaced a wooden
blower with a metal one, and why the *Degesch*
engineers proposed a metallic apparatus for the
disinfestation gas chamber with the *Kreislauf*
system, like those that appear on Documents 16
and 17 of his book. Why would they have done
this — so that they could have been "corroded" by
hydrocyanic acid?

In these rooms, standard or *normal,* which had a
volume of $10m^3$, one can of Zyklon B of 200g
(HCN contents) was used in order to produce a
gas concentration of $20g/m^3$. Pressac states, as
always without any proof, that this was the concentration of the alleged homicidal gas chambers.
But previously, he claimed that the concentration
of gas used in homicidal gas chambers of
Birkenau was $12g/m^3$.[83] We shall later learn the
reason for this increase.

Drahtnetzeinschiebvorrichtung does not signify
«dispositifs *d'introduction* en treillis de fil de fer»
["*introduction* devices made of wire netting"] (p.
79), but rather, *insertion* devices (the verb *ein-
schieben,* means in fact, "*insert, to slide into*"; for
example, one "*inserts*" a drawer in a closet).

The device for the *introduction* of Zyklon B in the
alleged homicidal gas chambers would be called
Einwurfvorrichtung (Pressac himself speaks in
fact of *déversement,* "pouring out," of the Zyklon B
in the alleged homicidal gas chambers [p. 89]).
The *Holzblenden, obturateurs de bois,* "wooden

obstructors" (p. 79), cannot be what Pressac maintains, i.e. wooden covers of the alleged introduction devices of the Zyklon B: These devices would be called in fact *Holzdeckel,* precisely *covers,* not *obstructors.*

Pressac states that the above-mentioned devices were found in "morgue 1" (p. 79), that is, in *Leichenkeller 1,* the alleged homicidal gas chamber. In reality, in the inventory of Crematory II,[84] these devices are attributed to Leichenkeller 2, the alleged changing room (for the supposed homicidal gas chamber): Did the SS want to gas the victims in the "changing room"? But that's not all! These devices do not figure at all in the inventory of Crematory III:[85] Then how did the SS think they could introduce the Zyklon B into the gas chamber? — by affably asking the victims to carry in the cans of Zyklon B and open them after the gas-proof door closed behind them?

Therefore, these devices could have been anything but what Jean-Claude Pressac claims.

- The designation *cave à déshabillage* "cellar for undressing" (p. 74), *Auskleidekeller,* attributed to Leichenkeller 2, is perfectly normal, from the moment that a temporary disinfestation gas chamber was installed in Leichenkeller 1.

Jährling's *bavure* shows once again, as if there were any more need for it, with what kind of distorted logic Pressac has fabricated his "criminal traces." The passage merits citation in its entirety; but first, it is necessary to give a brief historical setting. Nineteen Zyklon B gas disinfestation chambers with the *Kreislauf* system were designed for the *Aufnahmegebäude* (reception building of the new prisoners) of the main camp. The *Kreislauf* systems were not at first installed.

At the end of 1943, it was decided to transform eight of these rooms into short wave disinfestation chambers, in line with a new process developed by the Siemens company. Work began in February 1944 (p. 88). At the same time, it was decided to put the eleven remaining rooms into operation by installing the *Kreislauf* system. The Boos company, which should have performed this work, raised objections. The Testa company (Tesch und Stabenow), distributor of Zyklon B, had also taken an interest in the affair, as had Dr. Wirths, who remembered that according to an ordinance in effect, the Zyklon B had to be replaced by another gas: Areginal, the use of which required an adaptation of the Zyklon B gas chambers. (pp. 88–89).

> A cette occasion, l'employé civil Jährling commit une extraordinaire bévue dans une lettre destinée à la Testa. Il désigna les chambres a gaz d'épouillage de ‹Normalgaskammer› mot souligné et mis entre guillemet, comme s'il existait des chambres a gaz ‹normales› et d'autres ‹anormales›. L'appellation fut reprise par la Testa, qui affirmait d'abord que la conversion a l'Areginal n'était obligatoire que dans le cas d'installations nouvelles, et insistait surtout pour que le personnel s'occupant des chambres à gaz normales à l'acide cyanhydrique fût particulierement bien formé, sous-entendant que leur fonctionnement était nettement plus complexe que le simple *déversement* de Zyklon B dans des chambres a gaz ›anormales‹. (p. 89, our italics)

> [On this occasion, the civil employee Jährling committed an extraordinary blunder in a letter destined for the Testa company. He designated the delousing gas chambers as 'Normalgaskammer,' a word underlined and put in quotation marks, as if there existed 'normal' gas chambers and others which were 'abnormal.' The appellation was taken up by the Testa company, which first stated that the conversion to Areginal[*] was only obligatory in the new installa-

tions, and insisted that the personnel who handled the normal gas chambers with the hydrocyanic acid should be particularly well trained: implying that their operation was distinctly more complex than the simple *pouring* of Zyklon B into the 'abnormal' gas chambers.]

If Pressac had familiarized himself even a little with the disinfestation gas chambers using hydrocyanic acid, he would have known that a *Normalgaskammer* was a gas chamber according to the norms; that is, a standard *Degesch* room with a *Kreislauf* system. A disinfestation room not conforming to the norm was a simple auxiliary gas chamber (*behelfsmässige Blausäurekammer*).[86]

Therefore, Jährling simply wanted to underline that the envisioned transformation of the operating system referred to gas chambers planned as hydrocyanic gas chambers with the *Degesch-Kreislauf, normal,* and not to chambers without such a system, *abnormal,* like that of the BW 5b system of Birkenau. That's all.

---

* The gas in question called Areginal (Alkylformiat) was used together with Cartox for the disinfestation of silos against *calandra granaria* (grain weevil), a fearful grain parasite (H.W. Frickhinger, *Schädlingsbekämpfung für Jedermann* [Leipzig: Heilingsche Verlagsanstalt, 1942]; G. Peters, *Die hochwirksamen Gase und Dämpfe in der Schädlingsbekämpfung: Sammlung chemischer und chemischtechnischer Vorträge* [Stuttgart: Verlag von Ferdinand Enke, 1942], pp. 37–38 and 55–57).

Chapter Six

Bunkers 1 and 2

Before examining Jean-Claude Pressac's statements on Bunkers 1 and 2, it is well to specify that this designation (like those of "red house" and "white house") is not found either in the German documents or in the reports of the clandestine resistance movement of the period at Auschwitz; it has been created by postwar *eyewitnesses.*

Pressac states that Bunker 1, destined for mass extermination, went into operation at the end of May 1942 (p. 39), that is, as we have seen, even before R. Höss received from Himmler the alleged order for extermination of the Jews.

There exists no document on the existence of Bunker 1 (and 2) as homicidal installations. What Pressac says on the subject, as if it were certified historical truth, is in reality the simple result of extrapolation of testimonies which contradict each other on all essential points.[87] According to Pressac, Bunker 2 began its activity at the beginning of June 1942 (p. 41). Pressac describes the genesis of the installation as follows:

Non loin de Bunker 1, s'élevait une seconde fermette, crépie de chaux et d'une superficie de 105 m². La transformer en chambre à gaz était simple, l'opération ayant déjà été realisée au Bunker 1, et un demi-millier de personnes pourraient y tenir. Mais Höss voulut améliorer la ventilation. Il consulta Bischoff qui lui montra un article du Dr. G. Peters, le direct-eur de la Degesch (entreprise fabriquant le Zyklon-B), où était décrite une installation d'épouillage au Zyklon-B avec huit petites chambres a gaz de 10 m³ disposees côte à côte. (pp. 41–42)

[Not far from Bunker 1 arose a second little white-washed farmhouse with an area of 105 m². To trans-form it into a gas chamber was simple. The operation had already been realized at Bunker 1, and it could have held half a thousand people. But Höss wanted to improve the ventilation. He consulted Bischoff, who showed him an article by G. Peters, the director of the Degesch Company (the enterprise fabricating the Zyklon B), which described a delousing installa-tion using Zyklon B with eight little gas chambers of 10 m³ arranged side by side.]

The article, as Pressac himself informs us, had been requested by the Boos Company:

afin de s'en inspirer pour équiper le futur bâtiment de reception des detenus du Stammlager d'une batte-rie de 19 cellules d'épouillage à gaz semblables. (p. 42)

[in order to use it as a guide for equipping the future prisoner reception building of the Stammlager with a battery of nineteen similar delousing gas cells.]

Therefore the article concerned the nineteen hydro-cyanic acid disinfestation rooms with the *Kreislauf* system planned for the *Aufnahmegebäude*. The date of the request is 1 July 1942 (p. 103, note 135), that is, one month after the alleged beginning of the activity of Bunker 2. That this article (in which the plan for a *Degesch* gas chamber with the *Kreislauf* system published by Pressac as Document 16–17, which has been previously discussed) is presented as having been shown by Bischoff to Höss for the purpose of furnishing Bunker 2 with a ventilation system. It is not attested to by any document, and is the pure fantasy of Jean-Claude Pressac, who states, moreover, that no mechanical ventilation system was installed in Bunker 2.

Finally:

> furent construites dans la blanche chaumière [Bunker 2] quatres petites chambres à gaz d'environ 50 m^3 (sic), *placées en parallèle,* sans ventilation mécanique, mais orientées au mieux dans le sens du vent (nord-sud à Birkenau). (p. 42, our italics)

> [Four little gas chambers of about 50 m^3 [sic] were constructed in the white thatched house (Bunker 2). These were *placed in parallel,* without mechanical ventilation, but oriented in the best direction for the wind (North-South at Birkenau).]

The aim of Pressac's reasoning is quite clear. One of the criticisms made of his previous book regarding the alleged homicidal chambers is that, even though the Germans were at the forefront of technology in hydrocyanic disinfestation chambers, thanks to their invention of the *Degesch-Kreislauf* System, the Germans' homicidal gas chambers were technologically rather unsophisticated. Pressac must therefore establish in some manner a connection between the two types of systems, which he does in a crafty manner, asserting on the one hand that the transformation of Bunker 2 into a homicidal gas chamber had been done:

> *en s'inspirant des installations d'épouillage montées par la Degesch de Frankfurt/Main* (cellules placées en parallèle), (p. 115, our italics)

> [*emulating the delousing systems installed by the Degesch Company of Frankfurt/Main* (cells placed in

parallel),]

and furthermore, that the first homicidal gassing in Crematory II had been done with the introduction of 6 kg of Zyklon B, which:

> représente une concentration d'environ 20 g d'acide cyanhydrique par m³, *identique a celle preconisée par les dirigeants de la Degesch dans leurs cellules d'épouillage.* (p. 119, our italics)

> [represents a concentration of about 20 g of hydrocyanic acid per m³, *identical to that authorized by the directors of Degesch for their delousing cells.*]

Thus, the Bauleitung engineers would have drawn the least significant element from the article of G. Peters (and E. Wüstiger): the arrangement of the gas chambers *en parallèle* (in parallel). Even if it had been possible to install only one gas chamber with an area of 105 m² they would have installed four, with a total area of 50 m²,[*] an average 12.5 m² each! This was unnatural, inasmuch as Bunker 2 was destined for a *mass* extermination. It would have been an arrangement that would only have obstructed an extermination process. Lastly, it is not clear how the remaining 55 m² of the house would have been used.

Concerning the concentration of hydrocyanic acid: because the volume of Leichenkeller 1 (506 m³) would have been reduced to about 406 m³, after the removal of about 100 m³ occupied by the 1,492 bodies of the victims and the reinforced cement columns, the concentration obtainable with 6 kg of Zyklon B[†] would have been (6,000 : 406 =) about 14.8 g/m³, not 20.

Not bad: Pressac states authoritatively that the concentration of hydrocyanic acid in the alleged homicidal gas chamber was 20 g/m³. Here the second

---

[*] The indication of 50 m³ is obviously a printing error.

factitious connection between the *Degesch* disinfestation gas chambers and the alleged homicidal **gas**
chambers is created from thin air.

In the beginning, the SS had not foreseen **changing**
rooms for Bunkers 1 and 2; the victims undressed *en*
plein air (in the open air), but then:

> Bischoff demanda dans son second rapport le mon-
> tage, près des deux Bunker, de quatre baraques-écu-
> ries de bois comme vestiaire pour les inaptes. Chaque
> baraque coutait 15,000 RM. La demande fut formulée
> ainsi: ‹*4 Stück Baracken für Sonderbehandlung der*
> *Häftlinge in Birkenau / 4 Baraques pour [le] traite-*
> *ment spécial des detenus à Birkenau.*› (pp. 45–46,
> Pressac's italics)

> [Bischoff requested in his second report the construc-
> tion, close to the two Bunkers, of four wooden hut-
> stables for changing rooms for the unfit. The cost of
> each hut was 15,000 RM. The request was formu-
> lated thus: *'four huts for the special treatment of the*
> *prisoners at Birkenau.'*]

The report in question was written at the end of July
1942, during a full scale typhus epidemic. As we have
explained, the "special treatment *of the prisoners*" did
not have a criminal significance, but was a health
measure coming under the sanitary provisions taken
by the SS to arrest the epidemic.

There is no need to add that the relation of these huts
to Bunkers 1 and 2 is a purely arbitrary opinion by
Pressac and, as usual, has no documentary founda-

---

† This datum, in reference to the first alleged homicidal gassing in Crematory II, is pure invention by Jean-Claude
Pressac, because in this connection, there exists no document, and no witness affirms that on such an occasion, 6 kg
of Zyklon B were used. Pressac draws this datum from R.
Höss, who speaks in general of 5–7 cans of Zyklon B, of 1 kg
each (NI-034, NI-036).

tion.

The *Badeanstalten für Sonderaktionen* mentioned in the *Aktenvermerk* of 21 August 1942 (p. 52) had the same function; each had to be equipped with two three-chambered ovens of the simplified models, evidently to cremate infected corpses of prisoners who died of typhus.

Pressac believes he has found a *bavure* in a plan of the area of interest at Auschwitz-Birkenau:

> indiquant que la zone où se situaient les Bunker 1 et 2 et leurs fosses d'enfouissement était classée ‹Sperrgebiet/zone interdit› (legend of Document 21 and p. 52)
>
> [indicating that the zone where Bunkers 1 and 2 and their burying pits were situated, was classified a 'prohibited area.']

But this document bears the date of 2 June 1943, at which time the two bunkers had ceased their alleged activity two and a half months earlier, and the so-called "cremation pits" (which Pressac transforms for the occasion into *fosses d'enfouissement,* "burying pits") had been covered over and the earth leveled: What, therefore, did the SS want to hide in this zone?

Actually, the *Sperrgebiet* refers to the entire white area within the oblique hatching, and therefore *includes* the entire zone of the camp of Birkenau. The *Sperr*gebiet is clearly related to various *Lagersperren* (camp *closures*) decreed by Höss due to typhus: 10 July 1942 (p. 115), 23 July (p. 116), 8 February 1943 (p. 118). In June 1943, typhus still raged in the Gypsy camp at Birkenau, and in Sector BI cases of typhus were reported until the end of July (pp. 120 and 121).

In May-June of 1944, during the deportation of the Hungarian Jews to Auschwitz,

le Bunker 2 fut réactivé pour la circonstance pour de petits groupes, dont les corps étaient brûlés dans une fosse d'incinération de 30 m². (pp. 90–91)

[Bunker 2 was reactivated on occasion for small groups, whose bodies were burned in an incineration pit of 30 m².]

This is decidedly irrational. The SS would have supposedly equipped an extermination installation providing "a half thousand" corpses at a time with a cremation area, sufficient at the most for 50 corpses; that is, only a tenth of the actual needs. It is necessary to add furthermore, that the *eyewitness* M. Nyiszli speaks of two "cremation pits" which measured 50m x 6m (600m² altogether), and served 5,000 to 6,000 corpses per day.[88] In his preceding book, Pressac considers this witness credible. His only fault: He multiplied the numbers by 4![89] Yet, in the specific case, Pressac mentions a burning surface 20 times less than that declared by Nyiszli, and a cremation capacity, deducible from the area, 100 to 120 times less!

On page 147, suddenly a second pit appears, *plus petite* (smaller) than the first. Pressac introduces *this* to increase the capacity of Bunker 2 slightly, so as to justify *technically* the alleged extermination of the Hungarian Jews. This does not change anything we have demonstrated above.

Chapter Seven

Crematories IV and V

Pressac states that Crematories IV and V were dependent upon Bunkers 1 and 2 (p. 50), and assigned to them (p. 52).

This logistic arrangement was, to say the least, an unhappy one, given that the distance of the crematories (road distance) from the supposed Bunker 1 was about 800 meters, and from the supposed Bunker 2 about 900 meters. Therefore, the corpses would have to have been transported to the crematories by truck. If one considers that in Crematory I (according to Pressac) a more rational extermination procedure had already been worked out, one subsequently begun in all four of the other crematories of Birkenau — the placing of the homicidal gas chamber in the crematory — the planning of two "criminal" crematories not only without gas chambers, but even 800 to 900 meters away from the alleged homicidal gas chambers, is decidedly senseless.

Describing the genesis of these crematories, Pressac writes:

Quant au crématoire IV (et V), son premier dessin d'août 1942 n'en montrait que la partie incinératrice. A la mi-octobre, la Konrad Segnitz, chargée de sa toiture, le représenta avec ses dimensions définitives, la salle du four étant prolongée d'une vaste morgue de 48 sur 12 mètres (576 m²), indiquant son utilisation ‹en bout de chaîne›: le déshabillage et le gazage des victimes se situaient toujours au Bunker 2, mais les cadavres produits étaient déposés dans la morgue du crématoire IV pour y être incinérés. *Puis,* les SS cherchèrent à placer une chambre à gaz (chauffée avec un poêle) au centre du bâtiment, ce qui lui aurait donné la disposition logique suivante:

Vestiaire ⇨ Chambre a gaz ⇨ Sas ⇨ Salle du four a 8 moufles (p. 67, our italics)

[As for Crematory IV (and V), its first drawing of August 1942 showed only the incinerator portion. In mid-October, the Konrad Segnitz company, assigned to do its roofing, depicted in its final dimensions that the oven room was an extension of a huge morgue, 48 by 12 meters (576 m²), indicating that its function 'at the end of the sequence', which was the undressing and the gassing of the victims, was always situated in Bunker 2, but the corpses produced were deposited in the mortuary of Crematory IV to be incinerated. *Then* the SS tried to place a gas chamber (heated with a stove) at the center of the building, which would have given it the following logical arrangement:

Changing room ⇨ Gas chamber ⇨ Airlock ⇨ Oven room with 8 chambers.]

The drawing of the Segnitz company is **Plan 1361,** dated 14 October 1942.[90] "Then," according to that statement, the SS at that time, tried to install a homicidal gas chamber at the center of the building heated by a stove. This is false because the presence of a stove at the center of the building appears in **Plan 1678** from 14 August 1942, and Pressac comments on this as follows:

> The presence of a stove in the uncompleted room of
> Drawing 1678 is a formal indication that it was used
> for gassing.[91]

Thereupon, Pressac expounds the subsequent development of the plans for Crematories IV and V:

> Mais le vestiaire manquait. Edifier une baraque-écu-
> rie à l'extérieur compensait cette absence et donnait:
>
> Vestiaire ⇨ chambre a gaz ⇨ Morgue Sas ⇨ Salle du
> four a 8 moufles.
>
> Les crématoires IV et V ayant un rendement
> incinérateur moitié moindre que celui des II et III,
> leurs chambres à gaz devaient être plus modeste. Les
> SS conjuguèrent leur besoin de chambres à gaz de
> faible capacité (100 m^2) pour ‹traiter› de petits
> groupes de victimes à l'idée de marche alternative et
> établirent ainsi le 11 janvier 1943 le plan définitif du
> crématoire IV (et V). (p. 67)
>
> [But the changing room was missing. The building of
> a hut-stable compensated for this absence and gave:
>
> Changing room ⇨ Gas chamber ⇨ Mortuary ⇨ Air-
> lock ⇨ Oven room with 8 chambers.
>
> Crematories IV and V, having incineration yields half
> of those of Crematories II and III, were to have more
> modest gas chambers. The SS combined their need
> for gas chambers of lower capacity (100 m^2) for 'treat-
> ing' small groups of victims with the proposal for an
> alternative operation and thus established, on 11
> January 1943, the final plan of Crematory IV (and
> V).]

The simplified plan laid out by Pressac includes this
sequence: a changing room which serves two homicidal gas chambers (No. 1 and 2), each for 500 "unfit,"
a corridor, a mortuary room, an *Sas* (airlock) chamber,
and the oven room (p. 67).

He adds that:

> cette conception nécessitait la construction d'un ves-

tiaire extérieur, qui n'était pas indispensable par
beau temps, les victimes se déshabillant dehors (été
1944), mais l'était en hiver. Pour éviter de le bâtir, les
SS attribuèrent à la salle centrale une double fonc-
tion, de vestiaire et de morgue, en alternance. (p. 68)

[this conception necessitated the construction of an
outdoor changing room, which was not indispensable
in nice weather, the victims undressing outside (summer 1944), but was necessary in winter. To avoid con-
structing it, the SS assigned to the Central Hall a
double function of changing room and mortuary,
alternately.]

In summary, the criminal structure of Crematories IV
and V, «établi par les techniciens et les ingénieurs de
la *Bauleitung*» ["established by the technicians and
the engineers of the Bauleitung"], revealed itself as
"aberrant" (p. 68), only because «les techniciens et les
ingénieurs» ["the technicians and the engineers"] of
the *Bauleitung,* after having furnished (according to
Pressac) Bunkers 1 and 2 with two changing shacks
each, now, unexplainably, had to *éviter* (avoid) building a single shack near Crematories IV and V! For
what reason? Impenetrable mystery!

Pressac states that Crematories IV and V were each
equipped with *two* gas chambers of 100 m^2 each, in
total *200* m^2, which could hold altogether *1,000* people, with a density of *five people* per square meter. But
in his book *Auschwitz: Technique and Operation of the
Gas Chambers,* he writes:

> The floor area of the block of *three* gas chambers was
> *240* m^2 (4,800 m^{3*}). *2,400* people could therefore be
> squeezed in at a density of *ten* per square meter [!][92]
> (our italics)

Yet the third gas chamber suddenly reappears on page
147. For what reason, we shall see later. In the above-

---

* Printing error, for 480 m^3.

mentioned book, Pressac admits that the extermination system of Crematories IV and V was even more *"aberrant,"* even with his forcibly inflated oven capacities:

> It would take four [or] **five days** to cremate 2,400 bodies.[93]

Considering the maximum real capacity of the ovens, the cremation of 2,400 corpses would have required over twelve days. Inversely, to cremate 2,400 corpses in the course of one day would have necessitated 100 chambers instead of the existing eight.

The gassing technique imagined by Pressac is this:

> Le premier gazage fut *catastrophique.* Un SS devait, masque sur le visage, monter sur une petite échelle pour accéder a une ‹fenêtre,› l'ouvrir d'une main et de l'autre verser le Zyklon B. Sa prestation tenait du numéro d'équilibriste et devait être répétée six fois. (p. 76, our italics)

> [The first gassing was *catastrophic.* An SS man, mask on face, had to climb on a little ladder to access a 'window,' open it with one hand, and with the other, pour the Zyklon B. This feat was like a balancing act, and had to be repeated six times.]

Pressac forgets to add that the SS juggler would also have had to plead affably with the victims not to push him backwards, or grab him, or pull him in, while holding himself with one hand on the ladder. He would have had to extend his other hand inside the window (perched at 1.70 meters above the pavement) to pour a can of Zyklon B into the gas chamber!

Pressac's narration continues:

> Lorsque les portes étanches furent ouvertes pour évacuer le gaz, on s'aperçut que l'aération naturelle etait inefficace et il fallut *percer d'urgence une porte* dans le couloir nord pour provoquer un courant d'air.

(p. 76, our italics)

[When the air-tight doors were opened to evacuate the gas, it was perceived that the natural ventilation was ineffective and it was *urgently necessary to open a door* in the north corridor to induce an air current.]

The story of ventilation in Crematories IV and V is one of those tales which illustrates the silliness of Pressac's argumentation. In his book *Auschwitz: Technique and Operation of the Gas Chambers,* Pressac pretends to see this door *"urgently"* opened in the *north* wall of Crematory *IV* in a photograph[94] which shows only the *south* side of Crematories IV and V — not of Crematory *IV,* which appears clearly in the foreground, but rather of Crematory *V,* which is in the background partially obscured by trees. The south wall of Crematory V is so indistinct that one can make out a door in connection to the corridor only with a great deal of determination, and examination of the original photograph[95] shows that Pressac has mistaken for a door, shade produced by trunks of trees delimited at the bottom by lighter ground.

Prüfer, arriving at Birkenau the 18th or 19th of May,

> constata avec une tristesse feinte que la garantie du four du crématoire IV était expirée et qu'il ne pouvait plus réparer un four édifié avec des matériaux de second choix, estima néanmoins que ses chambres à gaz étaient encore utilisables à condition de les ventiler mécaniquement, empocha une commande de deux installations de désaération pour les crématoires IV e V se montant a 2.510 RM, et repartit le 20. (pp. 79–80)

> [stated with a feigned sadness that the warranty for the oven of Crematory IV had expired, and that it was no longer possible to repair an oven built with second class materials. He judged that the gas chambers were nevertheless still usable, on the condition that they be mechanically ventilated. He pocketed an

order for two ventilation systems for Crematories IV and V, amounting to 2,510 RM, and departed on the 20th.]

The source indicated by Pressac in note 247 (p. 107) is a «lettre et devis Topf du 9 juin 1943» ["letter and estimate from Topf of 9 June 1943"]. But in *Auschwitz: Technique and Operation of the Gas Chambers* he affirms, regarding this same source:

The author would point out that NOTHING in this letter indicates that the air extraction systems proposed for Crematories IV and V were for the gas chambers, and that they could on the face of it, only be for the furnace rooms.[96] (capital letters by Pressac)

Given that the ventilation systems were so urgent and essential for the good operation of the alleged homicidal gas chambers, one would have expected them to be installed immediately; here is instead what occurred:

Concernant ces dernières, la Topf, qui avait trouvé difficilement un moteur électrique adéquat, expédia quand même une des deux désaérations en petite vitesse le 21 decembre. Elle fut stockée au Bauhof le 1er janvier 1944 et laissée ainsi jusqu'en mai 1944. (p. 88)

[Concerning these last, Topf, who had found an adequate electric motor with difficulty, nevertheless quickly shipped by freight train one of the two ventilation systems on 21 December. It was put into storage at the Bauhof on 1 January 1944, and left as such until May 1944.]

Regarding this, Pressac adds:

L'installation de désaération, en magasin depuis janvier, fut montée en mai au crématoire V, dont le four fut jugé capable de fonctionner correctement. Pour les deux chambres à gaz et le couloir, représentant un volume de 480 m³ presqu'égal à celui des morgues des crématoires II et III, Schultze avait prévu une désaération de même puissance: une soufflerie No.450 avec un moteur de 3,5 CV extrayant 8,000 m³ par heure. (pp. 89–90)

[The ventilation system, which had been in storage since January, was installed in May in Crematory V, whose oven was judged capable of functioning correctly. For the two gas chambers and the corridor, representing a volume of 480 m³, Schultze had anticipated a ventilation of the same capacity, almost equal to that of the mortuaries of Crematories II and III: A ventilator, No.450 with a 3.5 CV motor, extracting 8,000 m³ per hour.]

Leichenkeller 1 (the alleged homicidal gas chamber of Crematories II and III) measured 483 m³ (p. 30) and had a ventilator capacity of 8,000 m³ per hour (p. 38), corresponding to 16.56 air changes per hour. Schultze had planned a ventilator for the *three* alleged homicidal gas chambers of Crematory V, which measured 480 m³, with a capacity of 8,000 m³/h of air, corresponding to 16.66 air exchanges per hour. Therefore, the two systems had the *même puissance* [same capacity].

We have already pointed out that the volume of Leichenkeller 1 was 506 m³, and not 483 m³, and that the ventilators of its system had a capacity of 4,800 m³/h of air, not 8,000, which corresponds to 9.41 air exchanges per hour, and not 16.56. Therefore, concerning Crematory V, according to Plan 2036, of 11 January 1943,[97] the three areas supposedly transformed into gas chambers measured respectively:

Table 6: Volume of the "gas chambers"

12.35 m x 7.72 = 95.3 m^2 x 2.20 = 209.6 m^3
11.69 m x 8.40 = 98.2 m^2 x 2.20 = 216.0 m^3
11.69 m x 3.50 = 40.9 m^2 x 2.20 = 40.9 m^3
Totals: 234.4 m^2 466.5 m^3

Here Pressac finds himself faced with another difficulty: Because the combined volume of the *two* gas chambers (which he mentions on pages 67 and 68) is 422.6 m^3, the ventilator, with a capacity of 8,000 m^3/h of air, would correspond to 18.93 air exchanges per hour. In other words, engineering specialists from the Topf company are supposed to have equipped ground-level rooms, provided with doors and windows (and which therefore would have been more easily ventilated), with a ventilating system proportionally more powerful than those of basement rooms, which were more difficult to ventilate! Then Pressac introduces the third gas chamber, and increases the total volume from 466.5 to 480 m^3 to deceptively obtain two ventilation systems *de même puissance* (of the same power).

On page 90, Pressac presents a plan which shows the:

> désaération des chambres à gaz du crématoire V, conçue par Karl Schultze en juin 1943 et monté en mai 1944.

> [ventilation of the gas chambers of Crematory V, designed by Karl Schultze in June 1943, and installed in May 1944.]

The source is not indicated, because it does not exist. This plan is in fact the simple fruit of Pressac's imagination. Furthermore it is a mistaken fruit, because the letter from the Topf company of 9 June 1943[98] mentions:

> die Ausführung der *gemauerten* Entlüftungskanäle
>
> [the construction of *walled* ventilation ducts],

while Pressac's plan shows *bare* pipes.

Chapter Eight

Conclusion

With this, we have arrived at the close of our critique of these Auschwitz books by Jean-Claude Pressac.

The 1979 declaration of French historians on Hitlerian extermination policies closed with the following axiom:

> Il ne faut pas se demander comment, *techniquement* un tel meurtre de masse a été possible. Il a été possible techniquement puisqu'il a eu lieu. Tel est le point de départ obligé de toute enquête historique sur ce sujet.
>
> [We must not ask ourselves how *technically* such a mass murder was possible. It was possible technically because it took place. Such is the obligatory point of departure for all historic investigation on this subject.][99]

Jean-Claude Pressac, however, wanted to study the crematory ovens and the alleged homicidal gas chambers of Auschwitz-Birkenau *technically*, although he lacked the required technical competence to undertake such a study. Nevertheless, Pressac had to accept the Revisionists' methodological principle, according to which, where testimonies and technology disagree, it is the latter which must prevail. He has applied that principle by reducing the number of the alleged victims of homicidal gassing, due precisely to its incompatibility with the capacity (craftily inflated by him) of the crematory ovens. In this manner, he has opened an irreparable leak in traditional historiography, because technology reveals the material impossibility of mass extermination at Auschwitz-Birkenau. If therefore, Pressac wants to be coherent in his technical stance, all that remains for him is to accept this conclusion. If he does not accept it, he can only go backwards, declaring, in acceptance of the appeal of the French historians, that one must not ask how such alleged mass extermination was technically possible.

In any case, one thing is certain: These Auschwitz books by Jean-Claude Pressac represent *the end of a legend.*

Notes

1. *L'Express*, 23–29 September 1993, p. 78 and 80.

2. These examples are sufficient to illustrate the technical competence of Jean-Claude Pressac:

    He thinks that "the temperature has to be raised to 27°C for hydrocyanic acid to evaporate" [J.C. Pressac, *Auschwitz: Technique and Operation of the Gas Chambers*, p. 375.], ignoring that evaporation of hydrocyanic acid can occur even below its boiling point (25.6°C), even at temperatures below 0°C [See in this connection: G. Peters, *Die hochwirksamen Gase und Dämpfe in der Schädlingsbekämpfung: Sammlung chemischer und chemischtechnischer Vorträge* [Stuttgart: Verlag von Ferdinand Enke, 1942], pp. 85–88.]

    Regarding the crematory ovens, Pressac presents an "Operation plan of a Topf oven with three chambers which was built in two models in Crematories II and III" [J.C. Pressac, *Auschwitz: Technique and Operation of the Gas Chambers, op. cit.*, p. 492. Based on the deposition of H.

Tauber, in which the gases of the gasogenes pass *around* the chambers: The *technical* basis of this plan is a translation error! (Pressac's two translators have translated the Polish preposition *przez*, (through), as *around*. The translation error is found on p. 489. The Polish text says: *przez obie boczne retorty* [through the two lateral chambers] (Archiwum Panstwowego Muzeum w Oswiecimiu [hereafter: APMO], Dpr.-Hd, 11a, p. 133).

3. Pressac, *Auschwitz: Technique and Operation of the Gas Chambers*, p. 264.

4. *Ibid.*, p. 183.

5. *Ibid.*, p. 97.

6. *Ibid.*, p. 183.

7. *Kostenanschlag* of Topf for KL Mauthausen of 1 November 1940. Bundesarchiv Koblenz (hereafter: BK), NS4 Ma/54.

8. Letter from Topf to SS-Neubauleitung KL Mauthausen of 6 January 1941. BK, NS4 Ma/54.

9. Letter from Topf to SS-Neubauleitung KL Mauthausen of 14 July 1941. Staatsarchiv Weimar, LK 4651.

10. *"Factors Which Affect the Process of Cremation: Third Session"* by Dr. E.W. Jones, assisted by Mr. R.G. Williamson. Extracted from: *The Cremation Society of Great Britain Annual Cremation Conference Report* 1975.

11. APMO, D-Z/Bau, nr. inw. 1967, p. 65.

12. Letter of H. Kori G.m.b.H. to SS-Sturmbannführer Lenzer, Lublin, of 23 October 1941. Archiwum Panstwowego Muzeum na Majdanku, sygn. VI-9a, vol.1.

13. APMO, BW 30/46, p. 18.

14. APMO, BW 30/46, p. 6.

15. On the Volckmann-Ludwig oven see:

   • Dipl. Ing. Volckmann, Hamburg, «Ein neues Einäscherungsverfahren,» *Zentralblatt für Feuerbestattung,* 1931;

   • Kurt Prüfer, «Ein neues Einäscherungsverfahren, Eine Entgegnung,» *Die Flamme,* 40 Jg., 1931;

   • Richard Kessler, «Der neue Einäscherungsofen System Volckmann-Ludwig,» *Zentralblatt für Feuerbestattung,* 1931;

   • Friedrich Helwig, «Vom Bau und Betrieb der Krematorien,» *Gesundheits-Ingenieur,* 54. Jg., Heft 24, 1931;

   • H. Wolfer, «Der neue ›Volckmann-Ludwig‹ - Einäscherungsofen im Stuttgarter Krematorium,» *Gesundheits-Ingenieur,* 55. Jg., Heft 13, 1932.

16. H.R. Heinicke, *VL-Kremationsofen Bauart Heinicke.* Summary of the sales kindly furnished by the H.R. Heinicke company of Stadthagen.

   The two Volckmann-Ludwig ovens installed in the crematory of Dortmund in 1937 are described in Herman Kamper, «Der Umbau der Leichenverbrennungsöfen und die Einrichtung von Leichenkühlräumen auf dem Hauptfriedhof der Stadt Dortmund,» *Gesundheits-Ingenieur,* 64. Jg., Heft 12, 1941.

17. R. Kessler, «Rationelle Wärmewirtschaft in den Krematorien nach Massgabe der Versuche im Dessauer Krematorium,» *Die Wärmewirtschaft,* 4.

Jg., Heft 8–11, 1927.

18. W. Heepke, *Die Leichenverbrennungs-Anstalten (die Krematorien)* (Halle a.S.: Verlag von Carl Marhold, 1905), p. 71.

19. R. Schnabel, *Macht ohne Moral: Eine Dokumentation über die SS* (Frankfurt/Main: Röderberg-Verlag, 1957), p. 351.

20. Dr. H. Frölich, «Zur Gesundheitspflege auf den Schlachtfeldern,» *Deutsche Militärärztliche Zeitschrift*, I, 1–4, 1872, pp. 109–110.

21. Kostenanschlag auf Lieferung von 2 Stück Dreimuffel-Einäscherungs-Öfen und Herstellung des Schornsteinfutters mit Reinigungstür of Topf 12 February 1942. APMO, BW 30/34, pp. 27–33.

22. W. Heepke, «Die neuzeitlichen Leicheneinäscherungsöfen mit Koksfeuerung, deren Wärmebilanz und Brennstoffverbrauch» *Feuerungstechnik*, 21. Jg., Heft 8/9, 1933.

23. List of the cremations of the crematory at Gusen (26 September–12 November 1941). Öffentliches Denkmal und Museum Mauthausen, Archiv, B 12/31.

24. D. Czech, *Kalendarium der Ereignisse im Konzentrationslager Auschwitz-Birkenau 1939–1945* (Reinbeck bei Hamburg: Rowohlt Verlag, 1989), p. 281.

25. H. Langbein, *Menschen in Auschwitz* (Wien: Europaverlag, 1987), p. 74.

26. APMO, BW 30/7/34, p. 54.

27. The numbers of the deceased are based on the *Leichenhallenbuch* {a} and on the *Sterbebücher* {b} for the male camp, on the documents of the clan-

destine resistance movement {c} revised and corrected for the female camp.

a. APMO, sygn. D-Au-I-5.

b. APMO, Φ 502-4.

c. APMO, Ruch Oporu, t. II, sygn. RO/85, p. 62, 62a.

28. APMO, D-Au-I-4, segregator 22, 22a.

29. This number is derived from the *Auschwitz Kalendarium*.

30. J.C. Pressac, *Auschwitz: Technique and Operation of the Gas Chambers*, p. 227.

31. *Commander at Auschwitz: Autobiographical memoirs of Rudolf Höss* (Turin: Einaudi, 1985), pp. 180. *Kommandant in Auschwitz. Autobiographische Aufzeichnungen des Rudolf Höss* ed. Martin Broszat (Munich: Deutscher Taschenbuch Verlag, 1981), p. 171.

32. J.-C. Pressac, *Auschwitz*, p. 132.

33. *Ibid.*, p. 183.

34. *Ibid.*, p. 183.

35. *Ibid.*, p. 236.

36. *Ibid.*, p. 236.

37. *Ibid.*, pp. 162 and 213.

38. *Ibid.*, pp. 236 and 390.

39. F. Piper, "Estimating the Number of Deportees to and Victims of the Auschwitz-Birkenau Camp." *Yad Vashem Studies* 21 (Jerusalem, 1991), 49–103; Auschwitz. *Wie viele Juden, Polen, Zigeuner...wurden umgebracht* (Krakow: Universitas,

1992).

40. R. Jakobskötter, «Die Entwicklung der elektrischen Einäscherung bis zu dem neuen elektrisch beheizten Heisslufteinäscherungsofen in Erfurt,» *Gesundheits-Ingenieur,* 64. Jg., Heft 43, 1941, p. 583

41. The crematory oven of Gusen went into operation on 29 January 1941. From February to October 1941 in the Gusen camp, 3,179 prisoners died. H. Marsalek, *Die Geschichte des Konzentrationslager Mauthausen. Dokumentation* (Vienna: Österreichische Lagergemeinschaft Mauthausen, 1980), p. 156.

42. *Bescheinigung über besondere Berechnung geleistete Tagelohn-Arbeiten,* 12 October − 9 November 1941. BK, NS4 Ma/54.

43. R. L. Braham, *The Politics of Genocide: The Holocaust in Hungary* (New York: Columbia University Press, 1981). See the summary table of the deportations on p. 602 of vol. 2.

44. *Records of the Defense Intelligence Agency* (RG 373). Mission 60 PRS/462 60 SQ, CAN D 1508, Exposure 3055, 3056.

45. J.C. Ball, *Air Photo Evidence* (Delta, B.C., Canada: Ball Resource Services Ltd.).

46. See in this connection: Carlo Mattogno, *La soluzione finale: Problemi e polemiche* (Edizioni di AR, Padova 1991).

47. *Commander at Auschwitz,* pp. 171–174; *Kommandant in Auschwitz,* pp. 157–159.

48. D. Czech, *Kalendarium der Ereignisse im Konzentrationslager Auschwitz-Birkenau,* in: *Hefte von*

Auschwitz, Wydawnictwo Panstwowego Muzeum w Oswiecimiu, 3, 1960, p. 49.

49. D. Czech, *Kalendarium der Ereignisse im Konzentrationslager Auschwitz-Birkenau 1939–1945,* p. 186.

50. *Ibid.,* p. 239.

51. *Ibid.,* pp. 117–119.

52. S. Klodzinski, «Pierwsza zagazowanie wiezniów i jenców w obozie oswiecimskim,» *Przeglad Lekarski,* I, 1972.

53. Pressac, *Auschwitz: Technique and Operation of the Gas Chambers,* p. 132.

54. Carlo Mattogno, *Auschwitz: La Prima Gasazione* [Auschwitz: The First Gassing] (Edizioni di AR, Padova 1992).

55. *Ibid.,* p. 159: "Since moreover the first gassing, according to the judge Jan Sehn, was an execution of condemnees to death selected by the commission presided over by Mildner, which arrived at Auschwitz 'in November 1941' and concluded its work 'after a month,' the first gassing in any case could not have occurred before December."

56. *Ibid.,* p. 85.

57. *Ibid.,* p. 84.

58. Pressac even presents his own drawing of such columns (*Auschwitz: Technique and Operation of the Gas Chambers,* p. 487).

59. Mattogno, *Auschwitz: La Prima Gasazione* [Auschwitz: The First Gassing], pp. 131–132. The reference is to the article by G. Peters and W. Rasch, «Die Einsatzfähigkeit der Blausäure-

Durchgasung bei tiefen Temperaturen,» *Zeitschrift für hygienische Zoologie und Schädlingsbekämpfung,* 1941.

60. *Ibid.,* pp. 28–29 and 36–37.

61. Pressac, *Auschwitz: Technique and Operation of the Gas Chambers,* p. 184.

62. The *Auschwitz Kalendarium* places this alleged order under 2 November 1944 (*op. cit.,* p. 921).

63. The mortality indicated by Pressac, based on the *Sterbebücher,* is lower than the actual, because these registers contain only a small portion of the deaths that took place among the female prisoners.

64. NO-2362, NO-2363; *Kalendarium der Ereignisse im Konzentrationslager Auschwitz-Birkenau,* p. 259.

65. Pressac, *Auschwitz: Technique and Operation of the Gas Chambers,* p. 188.

66. *Auschwitz vu par les SS [Auschwitz Seen by the SS]* (Musée d'Etat à Oswiecim [Oswiecim State Museum], 1974), p. 337. The WVHA was informed monthly of the number of prisoner deaths in all the concentration camps, including Auschwitz (PS-1469).

67. Pressac, *Auschwitz: Technique and Operation of the Gas Chambers,* p. 302.

68. *Ibid.,* p. 484.

69. Pressac, *Technique and Operation of the Gas Chambers,* p. 286.

70. APMO, D-Z/Bau, nr. inw. 1967, pp. 246–247 (see appendix, Document No. 2).

71. APMO, D-Z/Bau, nr. inw. 1967, pp. 231–232 (see appendix, Document No. 3).

72. Pressac, *Technique and Operation of the Gas Chambers*, p. 286.

73. Heepke, *Die Leichenverbrennungs-Anstalten*, p. 104 (see appendix, Document No. 4).

74. This follows, among other things, from the article by G. Peters and E. Wüstiger mentioned by Pressac on pages 41 and 103, from which he also draws Documents 16–17. The title indicated by J.C. Pressac: «Entlausung mit Zyklon Blausäure in Kreislauf-Begasungskammern» (*Zeitschrift für hygienische Zoologie und Schädlingsbekämpfung*, Heft 10/11, 1940) (note 134 on p. 103) is wrong; the exact title is: «Sach-Entlausung in Blausäure-Kammern» (*Zeitschrift für hygienische Zoologie und Schädlingsbekämpfung*, 1940, pp. 191–196). On page 195 one reads:

> Ventilator mit Motor. Für diesen ist eine Leistung von 12 cbm je Minute bei einem stat. Druck von 80 mm WS ausreichend, um sowohl eine äusserst rasche Gasentwicklung als auch eine genügend rasche Luftung (72-facher Luftwechsel je Stunde) des begasten Kammerinhalts zu bewirken.

> [Ventilator with motor. For this a capacity of 12 m³ per minute with a static pressure of 80 mm of water column is sufficient to produce a very rapid development of the gas as well as a sufficiently rapid ventilation (72 air exchanges per hour) of the contents of the gassed chamber.] (See appendix, Document No. 5 and 6.)

75. Pressac, *Auschwitz: Technique and Operation of the Gas Chambers*, p. 370.

76. *Ibid.*, p. 68.

77. APMO, nr, neg. 1034/7, p. 5.

78. F. Puntigam, H. Breymesser, E. Bernfus, *Blausäuregaskammern zur Fleckfieberabwehr.* Sonderveröffentlichung des Reicharbeitsblattes (Berlin, 1943), p. 31.

79. *«Hütte» des Ingenieurs Taschenbuch* (Berlin: Verlag von Wilhelm Ernst & Sohn, 1931), vol.1, p. 1013, No.3, with specific and exclusive reference to the *«Rauchgasanalyse»* (analysis of combustion gases) (p. 1011) (see appendix, Document No. 9).

80. «Blausäuregaskammern zur Fleckfieberabwehr», p. 21.

81. Letter of the Tesch & Stabenow company of 29 July 1942 to the *Waffen-SS Kriegsgefangenenlager Lublin, Verwaltung* (see appendix, Documents Nos. 10 & 11).

82. APMO, BW 30/25, p. 8.

83. Pressac, «Les Carences et Incoherences du ‹Rapport Leuchter›» [The Deficiencies and Incoherences of the 'Leuchter Report'], *Jour J,* 1988, p. III.

84. Übergabverhandlung of Crematory II, 31 March 1943. APMO, BW 30/43, p. 12.

85. Übergabverhandlung of Crematory III, 24 June 1943. APMO, BW 30/43, p. 24.

86. «Blausäuregaskammern zur Fleckfieberabwehr». This work describes with great accuracy two types of gas chambers: the standard ones with the «Kreislauf» system and the «Behelfsmässige Blausäurekammern» (pp. 62–68).

87. On page 59, Pressac writes regarding prisoners working at cremating corpses buried in common graves:

Ils étaient devenus, involontairement, les seuls témoins, en dehors des SS, des signes extérieurs du massacre des Juifs car, parmi les détenus qui participèrent à ce ›nettoyage‹, *aucun ne fut laissé en vie.* (our italics)

[They had become, involuntarily, the only witnesses, outside of the SS, of the outward signs of the massacre of the Jews, for among the prisoners that had participated in this 'cleansing', *none were left alive.*]

How, then, is the fact explained that the *eye witnesses* of the alleged extermination activity of the Bunkers were still left alive?

88. M. Nyiszli, *Médecin à Auschwitz: Souvenirs d'un médecin déporté,* traduit et adapté du hongrois par Tibère Kremer [M. Nyiszli, *Doctor at Auschwitz. Memories of a Deported Doctor,* translated and adapted from Hungarian by Tibere Kremer] (Paris: Julliard, 1961), pp. 96–98.

89. Pressac, *Auschwitz: Technique and Operation of the Gas Chambers,* p. 479. Actually M. Nyiszli is a false witness. See in this connection our study «*Medico ad Auschwitz*»: *Anatomia di un falso* ["*Doctor at Auschwitz*": *Anatomy of a Fake*] (Parma: Edizioni La Sfinge, 1988).

90. Pressac, *Auschwitz: Technique and Operation of the Gas Chambers,* p. 397.

91. *Ibid.,* p. 392.

92. *Ibid.,* p. 384

93. *Ibid.,* p. 384.

94. *Ibid.,* pp. 416–417

95. APMO, nr. neg. 20995/465.

96. Pressac, *Auschwitz: Technique and Operation of*

the Gas Chambers, p. 386.

97. *Ibid.,* p. 399.

98. APMO, BW 30/27, p. 18.

99. *Le Monde,* 21 February 1979, p. 23.

Appendix: Documents

About the documents

The technical documents included in this appendix refer to two important aspects of the presumed «machinerie de meurtre de masse» [machinery of mass murder] treated in this study: that of the ventilation of the Leichenkeller [basement morgue] of Crematories II and III, and that of the Gasprüfer [gas testers].

According to Pressac, Leichenkeller 1 is the presumed homicidal gas chamber. Documents 2 and 3 refute the affirmations of Jean-Claude Pressac, according to which the capacity of the ventilators of the ventilating system for Crematories II and III of Birkenau was 8,000m^3 of air per hour: the actual capacity was 4,800m^3 of air per hour, corresponding to 9.48 exchanges of air per hour.

These documents show, moreover, that the capacity of the *Entlüftung* exhaust ventilator of Leichenkeller 2 (the presumed dressing room) was 10,000m^3 of air per hour, corresponding to 11 exchanges of air per hour. The consequence is that, paradoxically, the Zentralbauleitung engineers of Auschwitz and the Topf engineers provided a lower number of air exchanges for the homicidal gas chamber than for the dressing room.

The number of air exchanges planned for these locations is in reality that which Engineer Wilhelm Heepke, one of the most specialized German engineers in the field of crematories, prescribed for morgue rooms destined for intense use (Document 4). Therefore, the Leichenkeller were projected and constructed as mortuary chamber morgues.

The warm-air circulation disinfestation chambers constructed by DEGESCH (DEGESCH-Kreislauf-Anlage für Entlausung mit Zyklon-Blausäure) had in effect a ventilator with a capacity of $12m^3$ of air per minute, corresponding to 72 exchanges of air per hour (Documents 5 and 6).

With this falls also the affirmation of Pressac according to which Leichenkeller 1 was transformed into a homicidal gas chamber. The fact that Crematories II and III, which were projected and constructed as plain hygienic-sanitary installations, entered into function with the same number of ovens and with the same capacity of the ventilators of Leichenkeller 1 projected from the very beginning, demonstrates that they were not transformed into «machinerie de meurtre de masse» [machinery of mass murder].

On 26 February 1943, the Zentralbauleitung of Auschwitz requested Topf to send ten *Gasprüfer* [gas testers](Document 7). The Topf company supposedly responded with a letter dated 2 March 1943 which speaks of *Anzeigegeräte für Blausäure Reste* [instruments for indicating remnants of hydrocyanic acid, or prussic acid] (Document 8). Jean-Claude **Pressac** attributes to this document the value of a definite proof of the existence of a homicidal gas chamber in Crematory II.

The *Gasprüfer* was a device for the analysis of burnt gases functioning according to physics (Document 9). The test kit for Zyklon B residual gas was called *Gasrestnachweisgerät für Zyklon* [apparatus which shows evidence of residual gas] (Document 10) and it functioned according to chemical methods; this was distributed by the same company which supplied the Zyklon B. *Gasrestnachweisgerät* came in a small wooden box containing:

1. eine Flasche mit Lösung I (2,86 Kupferazetat im Liter)

2. eine Flasche mit Lösung II (475cm³ bei Zimmertemperatur gesättigte Benzidinazetatlösung und 525cm³ Wasser)

3. Mischgefäss mit 2 Marken zum Abmessen gleicher Raumteile

4. Papprolle mit Fiesspapierstreifen

5. Farbmuster (Papierstreifen in Reagenzglas)

6. sechs leere dickwandige Reagenzgläser mit Korken.

[1. a bottle with Solution 1 (2.86g of copper acetate per liter)

2. a bottle with Solution 2 (475ml at room temperature of a saturated solution of benzidine acetate in 525ml of water)

3. a mixing utensil with two markers for measuring equivalent room areas

4. a cardboard roll with strips of blotting paper

5. color test pattern (strips of test paper in a test tube)

6. six empty thick-walled test tubes with cork stoppers]

The test for the residual gas *(Gasrestprobe)* was accomplished by mixing in the mixing utensil the required proportions of Solutions 1 and 2. In the solution thus obtained, one immersed the lower parts of six strips of blotting paper, each one of which was then introduced into a test tube which was quickly secured with a cork stopper. The person performing the test, wearing a gas mask, entered the area for testing with the test tubes which were opened at various locations exposing the strips of blotting paper which were moistened with the test solution. The paper strips reacted in the presence of hydrocyanic acid gas, taking on a blue coloration which becomes more intense with a higher concentration of the gas. [A. Sieverts, A. Hermsdorf, Der Nachweis Gasförmiger Blausäure In Luft. Zeitschrift Für Angewandte Chemie, 34. JG., 1921, pp. 4–5]

Document 11 is a photograph of a *Gasrestnachweisgerät* which was found by the Soviets at Auschwitz after the liberation of the camp.

Document 12 is an Allied serial photo of Auschwitz 31 May 1944. Also published in *The Ball Report* (Toronto: 1993), p. 5.

Document No. 1. The table of contents of a study entitled, *The Crematory Ovens of Auschwitz-Birkenau,* by Carlo Mattogno with the collaboration of Engineer Dr. Franco Deana, of Genoa, Italy.

Introduction

A. TOPF & SÖHNE, ERFU:.	Bauvorhaben:
chinenfabrik u. Feuerungstechnisches Baugeschäft	Haushalt: .... Kap.: .... Tit.: ....
llumm :.*Gesi*	Genehmigungsverfügung vom:
	Kostien (vor) anschlag vom:
	Auftrag Nr.: .... vom .... mit .... RM
	Vertrag Nr.: .... vom .... mit .... RM
:ril des Empfängers:	Bauwerk (BW)
die	Bauausgabebuch Seite: .... Nr.
:tral-Bauleitung der	Freihändige Vergebung
fen-SS und Polizei	beschränkte Ausschreibung · Z JUL. 1· 4
:chwitz / Ost-Oberschles.	öffentliche Ausschreibung

/ Teil- / Schluß-			Orı Erfurt, 27.5.43
hnung Nr. 729	Unser Hausnd 132	Unsere Auftrags-Nr. u. Zeichen 42 D 1520	Straße Havsnummer Dreysextr. 7/9
·e Reichsbetriebs-Nr.	Ihre bestehende Dienststelle	Bedarfsgruppe	Ihre Bestellung Nr. (Tag)
:swaren-Nr		Zeit der Leistung, Versandtag	
:dangeben			

Nr. des Kost.-An.	Gegenstand	Menge	Preis je Einheit	Betrag	Raum I. Vermerke
	Lieferung von Be- und Entlüftungs-anlagen wie sie im einzelnen in unserem Kostenanschlag v.4.11.42 beschrieben worden sind und zwar: A die Entlüftungsanlage für den B- Raum, bestehend aus:		... .-...		
	1 Gebläse zur Förderung von stündl. 4800 cbm Luft gegen 40 mm WS. Ge-samtpressung mit Drehstrommotor für 380 Volt, 50 Per. spritzwas-ssergeschützt, N = 2 PS., Motor-schutzschalter und Sterndreieck-schalter ohne Sicherung, 1 Frischluftansaugerohrleitung, 450 mm Ø, 1 Druckrohrleitung 450. mm Ø von der Gebläsedrucköffnung. bis zum gemauerten Kanal führend lt. Pos. 1 des gen. K.A.			720.--	
	B die Entlüftungsanlage für den B-Raum, bestehend aus:				
	1 Gebläse mit Motor und Zubehör wie vorstehend aunter A ausgeführt, 1 Abluftrohrleitung 450 mm Ø von gemauerten Abluftkanal bis zur Ansaugeöffnung des Gebläses führend, 1 Druckrohrleitung mit Wetterhaube lt. Pos. II des K.A.			1.127.--	(247)
	C die Einrichtungsanlage für den Ofenraum bestehend aus:				
		Übertrag:		1.847.--	

Document No. 2. J.A. Topf & Söhne, Erfurt. Billing No. 729 of May 1943 addressed to *Zentralbauleitung der Waffen-SS und Polizei Auschwitz* concerning Crematory III of Birkenau. APMO, D-Z/Bau, Nr. inw. 1967, pp. 246–247.

Nr	Nrl des Kost.-Art.	Gegenstand	Menge	Preis je Einheit	Betrag
				Übertrag:	1.847.--

1 Gebläse zur Förderung von stündl.
10000 cbm Abluft gegen 32 mm WS.
Gesamtpressung,
1 Drehstrommotor für 380 Volt, 50
Per. spritzwassergeschützt, N =
ca. 3,5 PS. mit Motorschutzschalter und Sterndreieckschalter,
1 Abluftrohrleitung mit einem ∅
von 550 bis 250 mm,
1 Druckrohrleitung mit Wetterhaube
lt. Pos. III d.K.A.   1.837.--

D die Entlüftungsanlage für den
Sezier-Aufbahrungs-und Waschraum
bestehend aus:

1 Gebläse zur Förderung von stündl.
3000 cbm Abluft gegen 20 mm WS.
Gesamtpressung mit spritzwasser-
geschütztem Drehstrommotor, N =
ca. 1 PS. mit Motorschutzschalter
und Sterndreieckschalter,
1 Abluftrohrleitung 375 mm ∅, vom
Abluftkanal zur Gebläsesaugöff-
nung, 1 Druckrohrleitung mit
Wetterhaube, 4 Abluftgittern mit
Jalousie-Klappenverschlüssen lt.
Pos. IV d.K.A.   779.--

E die Entlüftungsanlage für den
L-Raum bestehend aus:

1 Gebläse zur Förderung von stündl.
10000 cbm Abluft gegen 35 mm WS.
Gesamtpressung mit Spritzwasser-
geschütztem Drehstrommotor N =
ca. 5,5 PS., Motorschutzschalter
und Sterndreieckschalter, 1 Abluftrohrleitung, 1 Druckrohrleitung mit Wetterhaube lt. Pos. V.
des K.A.   3.332.--
Verpackung und Anfuhr   25.--
                                                           7.820.--

gem. uns. Schrb. v. 12.10.42 betr.
Ihre Bestellung v. 5.10.42 Beagb.
Nr. 14491/42/Jöh. (2. Anlage)

Ihre Zahlung:
2.2.1944   RM 7.820.--

(246)

Document No. 2. Continued.

A. TOPF & SÖHNE, ERFU...
maschinenfabrik u. feuerungstechnisches Baugeschäft

	Unterbelag Nr. ....
Bauvorhaben: ....
Haushalt: .... Kap.: .... Tit.: ....
Genehmigungsverfügung vom: ....
Kosten (vor) anschlag vom: ....
Auftrag Nr.: .... vom .... mit .... RM
Vertrag Nr.: .... vom .... mit .... RM

an des Empfängers:

die
tral-Bauleitung der
fen-SS und Polizei

chwitz / Ost-Oberschles.

Bauwerk (BW) ....
Bauausgabebuch Seite: .... Nr. ....
Freihändige Vergebung
beschränkte Ausschreibung
öffentliche Ausschreibung · 7 JUL. f. 4

Teil- / Schluß-				
nung Nr. 171	Unser Memorand 132	Unsere Auftrags-Nr. u. Zeichen 42 D 243	Ort Erfurt, 22.2.43. Straße Hausnummer Dreysestr. 7/9
Reichsbetriebs-Nr.	Ihre bestellende Dienststelle		Bedarfsgruppe	Ihre Bestellung Nr. (Tag)
veron-Nr.		Zeit der Leistung, Versandtag
angeben

r. des st.-Aa.	Gegenstand	Menge	Preis je Einheit	Betrag	Raum f. Vermerke
	über die Lieferung von Be- und Entlüftungsanlagen wie sie im einzelnen in uns.Kostenanschlag vom 4.11.41 beschrieben worden sind und zwar: A. die Entlüftungsanlage für den B-Raum, bestehend aus: 1 Gebläse zur Förderung von stündl. 4800 cbm Luft gegen 40 mm WS. Gesamtpressung mit Drehstrommotor für 380 Volt, 50 Per. spritzwassergeschützt, N= 2 PS, Motorschutzschalter und Sterndreieckschalter ohne Sicherung, 1 Frischluftansaugerohrleitung 450 mm ⌀, 1 Druckrohrleitung 450 mm ⌀ von der Gebläsedrucköffnung bis zum gemauerten Kanal führend lt. Pos.I des gen.K.A. B. die Entlüftungsanlage für den B-Raum, bestehend aus: 1 Gebläse mit Motor und Zubehör wie vorstehend unter A ausgeführt, 1 Abluftrohrleitung 450 mm ⌀ von gemauerten Abluftkanal bis zur Ansaugeöffnung des Gebläses führend, 1 Druckrohrleitung mit Wetterhaube lt. Pos.II d. K.A.			720.— 1127.—	
	Übertrag:			1847.—	232

Document No. 3. J.A. Topf & Söhne, Erfurt. Billing
No. 171 of 22 February 1943 addressed to *Zentralbauleitung der Waffen-SS und Polizei Auschwitz* concerning Crematory II of Birkenau.

Nr.	Nr. des Kost.-An.	Gegenstand	Menge	Preis je Einheit	Betrag
			Übertrag:		1847.-
		C. die Einrichtungsanlage für den Ofenraum, bestehend aus: 1 Gebläse zur Förderung vonstündl. 10000 cbm Abluft gegen 32 mm WS Gesamtpressung, 1 Drehstrommotor für 380 Volt, 50 Per. spritzwassergeschützt, N= ca. 3,5 PS., mit Motorschutzschalter und Sterndreieckschalter, 1 Abluftrohrleitung mit einem Ø von 550 bis 250 mm, 1 Druckrohrleitung mit Wetterhaube lt. Pos. III d. KIA.			1837.-
		D. die Entlüftungsanlage für den Sezier-Aufbahrungs-u.Waschraum bestehend aus: 1 Gebläse zur Förderung von stündl. 3000 cbm Abluft gegen 20 mm WS. Gesamtpressung mit spritzwasserge- schütztem Drehstrommotor, N = ca. 1 PS, mit Motorschutzschalter und Sterndreieckschalter, 1 Abluftrohrleitung 375 mm Ø vom Abluftkanal zur Gebläseansaugs- öffnung, 1 Druckrohrleitung mit Wetterhaube, 4 Abluftgittern mit Jalousie-Klappenverschlüssen lt. Pos. IV d.K.A.			779.-
		E. die Entlüftungsanlage für den L-Raum, bestehend aus: 1 Gebläse zur Förderung von stündl. 10000 cbm Abluft gegen 55 mm WS. Gesamtpressung mit spritzwasser- geschütztem Drehstrommotor N = ca. 5,5 PS, Motorschutzschalter und Sterndreieckschalter, 1 Ab- luftrohrleitung, 1 Druckrohrlei- tung mit Wetterhaube lt. Pos. V des K.A. Verpackung und Anfuhr gem.uns.Schrb.v.10.2.1942. Ihre Zahlungen: 7.4.1942 RM 4.000.— 4.2.1944 RM 3.820.— RM 7.820.—			3332.-- 25.-- 7820.--

Document No. 3. Continued

Verschlossen kann q_1 durch eine Jalousieklappe werden. Die Frischluft lässt sich durch Öffnen eines Fensters, welches in Höhe von q_1 liegt, genügend einleiten. Auf eine kräftige Lüftung ist ferner in den Leichenhallen Wert zu legen, um die Fäulnisvorgänge in den Leichen möglichst zurückzuhalten. Auch hier kommt es an erster Stelle mehr auf eine Entlüftung als auf eine Belüftung an. Die Leichen, bezw. die Särge sind nicht direkt auf den Fussboden zu legen, sondern hohl auf Böcken über denselben zu lagern, damit die Luft unterhalb der Leichen aus dem Raume abgezogen werden kann. Eine Zuführung frischer Luft erfolgt von oben. Man hat hier mindestens mit einem 5fachen stündlichen Luftwechsel zu rechnen; unter Umständen kann man sogar bei starker Benutzung des Raumes bis auf das 10fache gehen, welch hohe Luftabfuhr mit Hilfe eines Ventilators erreicht wird; vielleicht empfehlen sich gerade für diese Räume die neu aufgekommenen Uhrfeder - Ventilatoren. Die Luftkanalmündungen sind zur Abwehr der Insekten mit kleinmaschigen Drahtgittern zu versehen. Selbst bei höheren Aussentemperaturen ist eine künstliche Kühlung wegen der dann eintretenden starken Schwitzwasserbildung kaum nötig; im anderen Falle können den Leichen beigelegte Eisstücke den Zweck wohl ausreichend erfüllen. Bei der Bauausführung ist gerade bei diesen Leichenhallen auf eine Trockenlegung des Fussbodens, Abwaschbarkeit der Wände und guter Kanalisation bedacht zu sein. Gehört dieser Silo einem öffentlichen Kanalnetz an, so sind die Abwässer vor Eintritt in letzteres zu desinfizieren.

Im übrigen gelten hier dieselben Beziehungen wie bei den allgemeinen Lüftungsanlagen.

Die Beleuchtung kommt vorläufig noch als natürliche in Betracht, da die Benutzung der Krematorien infolge der geringen Zahl von Verbrennungen auf die Tageszeit beschränkt werden kann. Die Anordnung der Fenster, durch welche das Tageslicht in die Halle fällt, wie auch der Fenster der übrigen Räume, ist lediglich Sache des Architekten. Da in der Halle und in den zugehörigen Neben-

---

Document No. 4. Wilhelm Heepke, Die Leichenverbrennungs-Anstalten (die Krematorien). Verlag von Carl Marhold, Halle a.S., 1905, p. 104.

öffner betätigt, sodaß bei Beginn des Kreislaufes automatisch die in den Öffner eingesetzte Zyklondose entleert wird und deren Inhalt auf eine Unterlage fällt, die von der im Kreislauf geführten warmen Luft bestrichen wird.

Bei Einstellung des Vierwegeschalters auf „Lüftung" wird bei **geschlossenen Kammertüren** bei (D) **vorgewärmte Frischluft** angesaugt, mit der die ganze Kammer durchspült wird, bevor sie bei (A) zusammen mit der ausgespülten Blausäure wieder abgesaugt wird.

Ventilator mit Motor (2)

Für diesen ist eine Leistung von 12 cbm je Minute bei einem stat. Druck von 80 mm WS ausreichend, um sowohl eine äußerst rasche Gasentwicklung als auch eine genügend rasche Lüftung (72-facher Luftwechsel je Stunde) des begasten Kammerinhaltes zu bewirken.

Heizaggregat (9)

Dieses Heizaggregat erhält eine verschieden hohe Leistung je nachdem, ob es nur zur Beschleunigung der Gasentwicklung und Vorheizung der angesaugten Frischluft oder auch zur Erwärmung des gesamten Kammerinhaltes dienen soll.

Im letzteren Falle hat es 10000 WE zu liefern, die zu einer Erwärmung des Kammerinhaltes auf 30 bis 35° C innerhalb einer halben Stunde führen, auch wenn das Gut mit einer Temperatur von nur 5 bis 10° C in die Kammer hineingebracht worden ist. Bei der Lüftung erwärmt das Heizaggregat die angesaugte Frischluft auf mindestens die gleiche Temperatur, die der Kammerinhalt inzwischen angenommen hat, sodaß ein Niederschlag der Blausäuredämpfe vermieden und eine äußerst rasche Lüftung der Kleidungsstücke bewirkt wird.

Abb. 4.
Blausäurebegasungsanlage mit Kreislaufanordnung in Betrieb (8 Kammern)

Die etwa 70 bis 75 Minuten beanspruchende Gesamtbehandlung der Kleidungsstücke geht wie folgt vor sich:

Nach Einfahren des beladenen Wagens und Verschließen der Kammer (Abb. 4) wird der Ventilator (2) eingeschaltet und damit automatisch auch das Heizaggregat in Wirkung gesetzt. Der Vierwegeschalter (5), der bis dahin auf „Lüftung" gestanden hat und in dessen Gasentlüftungs-Einrichtung vor Verschließen der Kammer eine Zyklondose eingesetzt worden ist, wird nun auf „Kreislauf" gestellt. Mit dem dabei erforderlichen Drehen der Handkurbel wird die Zyklondose dadurch geöffnet, daß sich das Messer des Dosenöffners (1) vorschiebt und den Boden der Zyklondose

---

Document No. 5. G. Peters, E. Wüstiger, «Sach-Entlausung in Blausäure- Kammern,» *Zeitschrift für hygienische Zoologie und Schädlingsbekämpfung,* Heft 10/11, 1940, p. 195.

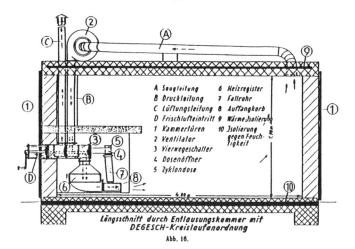

A Saugleitung	6 Heizregister
B Druckleitung	7 Fallrohr
C Lüftungsleitung	8 Auffangkorb
D Frischlufteintritt	9 Wärme Jsolierung
1 Kammertüren	10 Jsolierung
2 Ventilator	gegen Feuch-
3 Vierwegeschalter	tigkeit
4 Dosenöffner	
5 Zyklondose	

Längsschnitt durch Entlausungskammer mit DEGESCH-Kreislaufanordnung

Abb. 16.

Minutenleistung stammt, vermag innerhalb von 5 Minuten 60 v. H. des Blausäuregehaltes einer großen Zyklondose auszutreiben. Der restliche Doseninhalt von 40 v. H. ist in weiteren 10 bis 15 Minuten ausgetreten. Günstiger gestalten sich die Blausäureentbindungsverhältnisse bei Verwendung vorgewärmter Luft. Es ist verständlich, daß die über das Zyklon streichende Luft entsprechend der Blausäureverdunstung stark abkühlt. Während der Verdunstungsperiode sinkt die Lufttemperatur um 5 bis 10° C (Peters).

2. einem Ventilator mit Motor (2).

Der Ventilator hat eine Leistung von 12 m³ pro Minute bei einem statischen Druck von 80 mm WS und ist in seiner Leistung so gewählt, daß sowohl eine äußerst rasche Gasentwicklung als auch eine genügend rasche Lüftung (72facher Luftwechsel je Stunde) des begasten Kammerinhaltes damit erfolgt.

3. einer Kreislaufleitung (A-B);

4. einer Lüftungsleitung (A-C);

5. einer Frischluftzufuhr (D), kombiniert mit dem Vierwegeschalter.

Bei Einstellung des Vierwegeschalters auf »Lüftung« wird bei geschlossenen Kammertüren bei D Frischluft angesaugt, mit der die ganze Kammer durchspült wird, bevor sie bei A zusammen mit der ausgespülten Blausäure wieder abgesaugt wird.

6. einem Heizaggregat (6).

Document No. 6. F. Puntigam, H. Breymesser, E. Bernfus, *Blausäurekammern zur Fleckfieberabwehr.* Sonderveröffentlichung des Reicharbeitsblattes (Berlin, 1943), p. 50.

Telegramm

Anschr.: Topfwerke Erfut

Text: Absendet sofort 10 Gauprüfer wie besprochen. Kostenangebot später nachreichen.

84.00

Zentralbauleitung Auschwitz
gez. Pollok
ỷ-Untersturmführer

26.2.43 18²⁰

Document No. 7. Telegram of the *Zentralbauleitung Auschwitz* to the Firm
J.A. Topf & Söhne, Erfurt, of 26 February 1943. APMO, BW 30/34, p. 48.

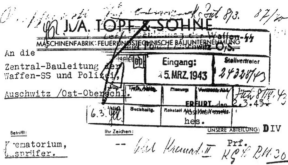

An die

Zentral-Bauleitung der
Waffen-SS und Polizei,

Auschwitz /Ost-Oberschl.

	Eingang:	Stellvertreter
	15. MRZ. 1943	

ERFURT, den 2.3.43

hes.

UNSERE ABTEILUNG: D IV

Betrifft:

Krematorium,
Gasprüfer.

Ihr Zeichen:

Prf.

Wir bestätigen den Eingang Ihres Telegrammes,
lautend:

" Absendet sofort 10 Gasprüfer wie besprochen
Kostenangebot später nachreichen ".

Hierzu teilen wir Ihnen mit, dass wir bereits
vor 2 Wochen bei 5 verschiedenen Firmen die
von Ihnen gewünschten Anzeigegeräte für
Blausäure-Reste angefragt haben. Von 3 Firmen
haben wir Absagen bekommen und von 2 weiteren
steht eine Antwort noch aus.

Wenn wir in dieser Angelegenheit Mitteilung er-
halten, kommen wir Ihnen sofort näher, damit
Sie sich mit einer Firma, die diese Geräte
baut, in Verbindung setzen können.

H e i l   H i t l e r !

J. A. TOPF & SÖHNE

ppa.

I.V.

Erledigt durch Schreiben

vom _____194_ Bftgb. Nr.

Reichsbank-Giro-Konto 75/851 — Postscheck-Konto Erfurt 1792
Telegramme: Topfwerke — Fernsprecher: Sammelnummer 251 25

Document 28 : Lettre de la Topf à la ZBL d'Auschwitz du 2 mars 1943 (ACM, dossier 502-1-313).

Document 27 (page précédente en bas) : Photo de la façade sud du crématoire II à Birkenau avec la cheminée collective des ventilations en construction. Au premier plan, sa cave à cadavres 1 (future chambre à gaz) semi-enterrée non encore équipée des ouvertures de versement du Zyklon-B. Les fours sont chauffés comme le montre la partie centrale du toit sans neige (APMO, nég. n° 20 995/506).

Document No. 8. J.A. Topf & Söhne, Erfurt. Letter of 2 March 1943 to the *Zentralbauleitung der Waffen-SS und Polizei Auschwitz*. J.C. Pressac, *Les Crématoires d'Auschwitz: La maschinerie du meurtre de masse* (Paris: CNRS Editions, 1993), Document 28.

Sättigungsdruck zu $t_1 : p_{S_1} = 6{,}25$ mm QS,

zu $t_1' : p_{S_1'} = 5{,}55$ mm QS,

Dampfdruck $P_{d_1} = 5{,}55 - 0{,}5 \cdot (4{,}35 - 2{,}65) = 4{,}70$ mm QS,

Relative Feuchtigkeit $\varphi_1 = 4{,}70 : 6{,}25 = 0{,}752$,

Sättigungsdichte zu $t_1 : \gamma_{S_1} = 6{,}52$ g/m³,

Spez. Gw des Dampfanteils $0{,}752 \cdot 6{,}52 = 4{,}91$ g/m³,

Dampfmenge $D_1 = 24\,500 \cdot 0{,}004\,91 = 120{,}2$ kg/h,

Relative Feuchtigkeit $\varphi_2 = 1$,

Sättigungsdichte zu $t_2 : \gamma_{S_2} = 4{,}23$ g/m³ $= \gamma_{d_2}$,

Volumen $V_2 = 26\,100 \cdot (735{,}5/754) \cdot (271{,}25/288) = 24\,000$ m³/h,

Dampfmenge $D_2 = 24\,000 \cdot 0{,}004\,23 = 101{,}5$ kg/h,

Niedergeschlagene Dampfmenge $D_1 - D_2 = 18{,}7$ kg/h,

Verdampfungswärme um 0° herum $r = 595$ kcal/kg,

Wärmebindung für Dampf $18{,}7 \cdot 595 = 11\,100$ kcal/h,

Gesamte Wärmebindung $45\,500 + 11\,100 = 56\,600$ kcal/h.

Vernachlässigungen dieses Rechnungsganges: Volumverminderung durch Verschwinden des Dampfvolumens, sowie Einfluß des Dampfanteils auf spez. Wärme sind nur bei geringen Dampfgewichten im Vergleich zum Luftgewicht zulässig, also nicht immer bei höheren Temperaturen (Trockenanlagen) oder bei niederen Drücken (Kondensationsanlagen, Vakuumtrockenanlagen), hier muß man nötigenfalls auf die Teildrücke für Luft zurückgehen.

Wärmeverlust durch Isolierungen mißt man nach der Hilfswandmethode mit Wärmebinde von Hencky-Schmidt (Forschungsheim für Wärmeschutz, München). Hencky, Gesund. Ing. 1919, S. 496; Schmidt, Arch. Wärme 1924, S. 9.

VI. Feuerungstechnische Messungen
A. Heizwertbestimmung

Oberer und unterer Heizwert S. 572 u. 897. Unterer in erster Linie für Arbeitserzeugung maßgebend, oberer für Wärmeübertragung; doch kann eine Zahl nicht alle Eigenschaften des Brennstoffs kennzeichnen. Es ist $\mathfrak{H}_u = \mathfrak{H}_o - 600\,w$, worin w die aus 1 kg Brennstoff entwickelte (auch wohl schon als Feuchtigkeit darin enthaltene) Feuchtigkeitsmenge ist.

1. Bomben-Kalorimeter für feste Brennstoffe. Gewogene Menge in der Berthelot-Mahlerschen Bombe mit verdichtetem Sauerstoff verbrannt. Aus der Temperaturzunahme des Kalorimeters berechnet sich oberer Heizwert. Um den unteren zu finden, ist entweder die Krökersche Bombe zu benutzen, die die Messung des Verbrennungswassers gestattet, oder es ist die Elementaranalyse des Brennstoffs zu machen.

Die genaueste Kalorimetrierung ist zwecklos, wenn nicht sorgsamst eine Probe zubereitet wird, die Mittelwert der zu untersuchenden Lieferung darstellt; da Größenordnung beider, z. B. 1 g gegen eine Kahnladung, sehr verschieden ist, so kann nur fortgesetzte Halbierung oder Viertelung einer größeren Probe unter immer wieder eingehaltenem Durchmischen und unter Berücksichtigung des anfallenden Staubes zu brauchbaren Ergebnissen führen. — Einfluß hat auch Vermahlung oder Zerkleinerung: Eisengefäße ergeben Abrieb, der mit verbrennt und Asche vermehrt. — Man unterscheide: Heizwert der angelieferten (oft zufällig feuchten), der lufttrockenen Kohle, der brennbaren Substanz. Bei gleicher Herkunft pflegt letzterer etwa konstant zu sein, so daß für Regellieferungen die Bestimmung von Feuchtigkeit und Asche zur Umrechnung genügt.

2. Junkers-Kalorimeter für flüssige und gasförmige Brennstoffe. Eine durch Wägen bestimmte Menge flüssigen Brennstoffs bzw. eine durch Gasuhr gemessene Gasmenge wird verbrannt. Aus Menge und Temperaturzunahme des gleichzeitig durch das Kalorimeter fließenden Wassers ist Heizwert des Brennstoffs zu berechnen. Gleichzeitig wird etwas länger wird das gebildete Verbrennungswasser aufgefangen. — Union-Kalorimeter für einfachere Zwecke recht brauchbar; Vergleich des oberen Heizwertes mit gleicher Menge Knallgas; dessen Heizwert (für $H_2 + O$) ist 2020 kcal/m³ (0° u. 760 mm QS).

Document No. 9. "Hütte" des *Ingenieurs Taschenbuch* (Berlin: Verlag von Wilhelm Ernst & Sohn, 1931), vol.1, pp.1010–1013.

3. Heizwertbestimmung durch chemische Untersuchung (Notbehelf). Heiz-stoffe werden analysiert und Heizwert nach der **Verbandsformel** S. 574 aus den Analysenwerten berechnet.

B. Technische Gasanalyse[1])

Aus O_2 der Luft wird beim Durchgang durch Koks zunächst CO_2, bei längerem Weg (höherer Schicht) auch CO; Ergebnis: Rauchgase aus CO_2, O_2, CO, N_2, bezeichnet prozentisch mit k, o, c, n %. Bei Verbrennung von Kohle werden während der Entgasungszeit Kohlenwasserstoffe frei, die mit Luft zu CO_2 und H_2O verbrennen sollen; prozentische Menge des letzteren sei w %.

Rauchgasanalyse liefert k, o und c in Hundertteilen der trocken gedachten Gase; also ist $k + o + c + n$ $= 100$ %; Gesamtvolumen der heißen Rauchgase, in denen H_2O noch dampf-förmig ist, ist $100 + w$ gesetzt. Weil das durch Verbrennung von H gebildete H_2O volumetrisch beim Abkühlen verschwindet, steigt n über 79 % hinaus, N_2 nimmt scheinbar zu; am meisten, wenn bei vollkommener Verbrennung ohne Luft-überschuß das Rauchgasvolumen das kleinstmögliche ist und Rauchgase nur CO_2 und N_2 enthalten, wobei ebenso wie n

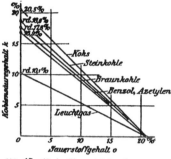

Abb. 17. Nachprüfung der Rauchgasanalysen.

auch k den größtmöglichen Wert annimmt, abhängig vom Gehalt an freiem, d. h. nicht durch Sauerstoffgehalt ausgeglichenem H_2, genauer vom Verhältnis C : H_2 (andere Bestandteile wie S vernachlässigt). Diese größtmöglichen Werte sind (Abb. 17) für:

Kohlenstoff mit C : $H_2 = \infty$		max $n = 79$	max $k = 21$
Koks	94	79,5	20,5
Steinkohle	21	81,9	18,8
Braunkohle	16	82,2	17,8
Acetylen, Benzol	12	83,1	16,9
Leuchtgas	2,2	9,9 %	10,1 %

max k entsteht, wenn die stöchiometrisch erforderliche Luftmenge L_0 zur Ver-brennung zugeführt wird, besser gesagt, wenn die durchgesaugte Luft so lange (Schichthöhe!) an Kohlenstoff vorbeigeführt wird, bis gerade aller O_2 in CO_2 verwandelt ist. Unter anderen Umständen, z. B. bei niedrigerer Schicht, bleibt O_2 neben CO_2 in den Gasen, es ist mehr Luft durchgesaugt, als für die verbrannte Kohle erforderlich, nämlich L statt L_0; das Verhältnis $L : L_0 = l$ heißt Luft-überschußzahl; man berechnet sie aus Analysenergebnissen mit den Formeln

$$l = n : \left[n - \frac{79}{21}\left(o - \frac{c}{2} \right) \right]$$
(genau, sofern Brennstoff keinen N_2 enthält; für Luftgas unbrauchbar)

$$l = \max k/k = 21/[21 - o]$$
(genau für reinen C, für Koks und Steinkohle noch brauchbar)

1. Orsat-Apparat zur Untersuchung der Heizgase von Kesselfeuerungen. 100 RT Heizgase werden nacheinander mit Flüssigkeiten, die CO_2, O_2 und CO absorbieren, in Berührung gebracht. Die Raumverminderung nach Absorption

[1]) Mitt. 123 u. 129 der Wärmestelle des Ver. d. Eisenhüttenleute; Ott in GWF 1926, 1929, Monatsbulletin der Schweiz. Ver. v. Gas- und Wasserfachmännern 1926, 1928.

64*

Document No. 9. Continued

Appendix: Documents

1012 I. Bd. 7. Abschn.: Meßkunde. VI Feuerungstechnische Messungen

gibt unmittelbar den Prozentgehalt an. Der Rest gilt als N_2. Zur Vermeidung von Temperatureinflüssen bei der Messung: Wassermantel um das Meßrohr. Temperaturausgleich nach Neufüllung usw. abwarten oder herbeiführen. Richtige Teilung der Bürette, Dichtheit der Schlauchverbindungen und Hähne prüfen. Ein Fehler kommt aus dem schädlichen Volumen der Verbindungsrohre; deren Raum soll kapillar sein, die Schläuche sollen ganz von aneinanderstoßenden Rohrenden gefüllt sein, die Hälfte des noch vorhandenen Volumens ist zum Bürettenvolumen hinzuzuzählen, am besten bei deren Teilung zu berücksichtigen. Oder Verfahren von Ott, a. a. O. 1928. Das Wasser säure man mit Schwefelsäure an und färbe mit Methylorange, um KOH, das in die Kapillaren gekommen sein könnte, unschädlich und kenntlich zu machen.

Zur Gasentnahme wird ein Rohr, bei höheren Temperaturen ($> 500°$) ein Porzellanrohr, bei hohen ein kaltwarmes Rohr (Kapillarrohr mit Wasserkühlung) verwendet, das durch das Kesselmauerwerk in den Feuerraum (für Untersuchung der Verbrennung) oder in den Fuchs (zur Feststellung der Essenverluste, s. II. Bd., Abschn. Dampferzeugung) bis Mitte Gasstrom hineinragt. — In die Leitung ein Rußfilter aus Glaswolle. Auf Dichtigkeit der Schlauchleitung achten!

Absorptionsmittel für

CO_2: Kalilauge, Rel.Gw 1,24 bis 1,32 (1 GT KOH auf 2 bis 3 GT Wasser)

O_2: Pyrogallussäure, 5 g heiß gelöst in 15 cm³ Wasser, dazu gemischt 120 g Ätzkali, gelöst in 80 cm³ Wasser; zulässiger Absorptionswert nur $2^1/_4$ cm³ O_2. Deswegen bequemer: Phosphorstengelchen unter destilliertem Wasser statt des Glasrohre in das Gefäß des Orsatapparates eingeführt; Absorptionswert sehr groß

CO: Ammoniakalische Kupferchlorürlösung: 250 g NH_4Cl gelöst in 750 cm³ Wasser, dazu 200 g Cu Cl (Vorratslösung, mit gutem Gummistopfen lange haltbar, wenn Kupferspirale darin). Zum Gebrauch $1/_3$ des Volumens Ammoniakflüssigkeit, Rel. Gw 0,91 hinzu. Zulässiger Absorptionswert 4 cm³ CO; oder: Cuprosulfat- β Naphthol-Suspension, Mitt. 129 der Wärmestelle des Ver. d. Eisenhüttenleute; oder: Jodpentoxyd nach Schläpfer u. Hoffmann, Bericht 25 der Fidgen. Materialprüfungsanstalt Zürich: 25 g feinstgepulvertes Jodpentoxyd werden mit 100 bis 150 g $10^0/_0$ Oleum in 3 bis 4 Portionen in einer Reibschale zu möglichst homogenem feinem Brei angerieben. Die gut aufgerührte Suspension gießt man vom gröberen, in der Schale zurückbleibenden Jodpentoxyd ab und verreibt es mit einem Teil der abgegossenen Suspension weiter, bis alle (!) Teile fein sind. Dann verdünnt man die Suspension mit 120 g desselben $10^0/_0$ Oleums und schüttelt die Mischung während einiger Stunden in einer Flasche auf der Schüttelmaschine. Richtig hergestellt[1], setzt die Suspension das Pentoxyd nur langsam ab und läßt es sehr leicht wieder aufrühren. (Mehr oder weniger als $10^0/_0$ SO_3 in Schwefelsäure ergibt Unregelmäßigkeiten: grobe Flötken, Kristalle.) CO wird in CO_2 verwandelt, dieses in der Kalipipette absorbiert. — Während Kupferchlorür wegen kleinen Absorptionswertes und loser Bindung manche Not macht, soll nach mehrfacher Auskunft J_2O_5 gut und zuverlässig arbeiten, zumal für größere CO-Gehalte.

Nachprüfung der Analysen: Man trage für alle Analysen $k = f (o)$ auf (Abb. 17); die Punkte müssen für einen Brennstoff auf eine Gerade fallen, die auf der Ordinatenachse max k abschneidet und anderseits nach $o = 21^0/_0$ geht. Die Punkte streuen, wenn im Lauf der Beschickungsperiode der H_2-Gehalt sich ändert, unvollkommene Verbrennung läßt Punkte tiefer fallen.

2. Selbsttätige Gasanalysatoren dienen zur dauernden Betriebsüberwachung. Ein Gasstrom wird dauernd dem Feuerzug entnommen und durch Gasanalysator geführt. Hier werden abgemessene Raumteile in regelbaren Zeitabständen durch Kalilauge hindurch unter eine kleine Meßglocke gedrückt. Hub der Meßglocke wird aufgezeichnet; er wird um so größer, je weniger Kohlensäure das Gas enthalten hat, d. h. je mehr der Gasprobe nach erfolgter Absorption von CO_2 unter die Meßglocke tritt. Meistens nur Bestimmung von CO_2; sog. Duplex-Apparate bestimmen auch CO. Beachte: Kurze Rohrleitungen und kurze Dauer der Analyse, um Nacheilung der Anzeige zu verringern; dichte Rohrleitungen, geschweißt oder aus Kupfer gelötet; kräftige Ansaugeeinrichtung (Quecksilberpumpe bei Maihak);

---

[1] Fertig bei Schildknecht, Zürich 7.

Document No. 9. Continued

Sichtbarkeit der Ergebnisse für den Heizer, anderseits Unbeeinflußbarkeit; Übertragung der Ergebnisse zum Heizerstand (S & H, neuerdings andere). Einfacher: Aspirator durch Wasserabfluß oder Glocke durch Uhrwerk (Dittmar & Vierth, Hamburg) während einer Betriebsschicht allmählich voll Gas saugen lassen und mittels Orsat durchschnittliche Zusammensetzung der Gase feststellen, z. B. für Heizerprämien.

Selbsttätige Analysatoren werden neuerdings auch für anderweitige Gasuntersuchung verwendet, etwa um SO_2 festzustellen; jeweils bestimmte Absorptionsflüssigkeit. Integrierung verlorener Kleinmengen durch Gasverlustwaage der Junkers-Thermotechnik.

3. **Gasprüfer** nach physikalischen Methoden nutzen Eigenschaften der Gase, die vom CO_2-Gehalt abhängen: RelGw ($CO_2 = 1,52$ gegen Luft $= 1$), Wärmeleitfähigkeit (60 gegen 100), Zähigkeit (1,5 gegen 1,7), Verhältnis spez. Gw zu Zähigkeit (etwa 2 zu 1), Brechungszahl (450 gegen 295). Vorteil gegen Analysatoren: keine Kalilauge, Anzeige sofort, vielfach bequeme Fernübertragung (zum Heizerstand); Nachteil: Beeinflussung durch Anwesenheit weiterer Gase, besonders H_2 und CH_4 sowie durch Temperatur und Feuchtigkeit. Gasprüfer von S & H (Leitfähigkeit), Ranarex der AEG, Unograph der Union Apparatebau-Gesellschaft Karlsruhe (Zähigkeit). Einfluß der Feuchtigkeit muß durch Trocknen oder durch Sättigen beseitigt werden.

4. **Der Kraftgasanalyse** dienen ähnliche Einrichtungen, namentlich erweiterte Orsat-Apparate, die noch schwere Kohlenwasserstoffe (Absorption mit rauchender Schwefelsäure), sowie CH_4 und H_2 ermitteln. Reihenfolge: Man läßt CO_2 absorbieren, dann schwere Kohlenwasserstoffe, O_2 und CO; Luft beigemengt, Verbrennung in Drehschmidts Platinkapillare, hierbei eintretende Raumminderung $\varDelta$ bedeutet $H_2 = \frac{2}{3} \varDelta$ oder $CH_4 = \frac{1}{2} \varDelta$; waren H_2 und CH_4 vorhanden, dann neugebildete CO_2 absorbieren, es war $CH_4 = CO_2$, es bleibt $H_2 = \frac{2}{3} \cdot (\varDelta - 2 CO_2)$.

Document No. 9. Continued

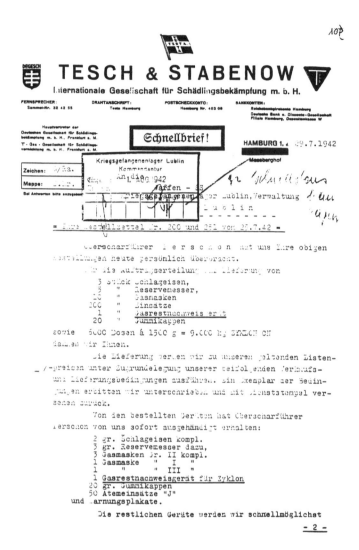

Document No. 10. Tesch & Stabenow, Hamburg. Letter of 29 July 1942 to the *Waffen- SS Kriegsgefangenenlager Lublin, Verwaltung.* Archiwum Panstwowego Muzeum na Majdanku, sygn. I d 2, vol. 1, p. 107.

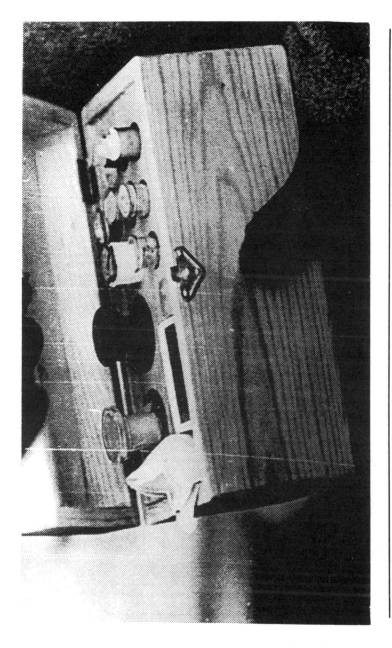

Document No. 11. APMO, photograph from Nr.neg.625. The *Gasrestnachweis-gerät für Zyklon* test kit.

Document No. 12. Allied aelial reconnaissance photograph of Auschwitz, 31 May 1944. No traces! National Archives (Washington, DC). RG 373. Exposure 3056. See note 44 on page 96; also page 32 of this book.

Glossary

A

Aide: A military officer acting as assistant to a superior

AL: Arbeitslager, work camp

Aktenvermerk: File entry

Alimentation: Allowance

Aleatorie: Co-incidental

Amtsgruppe: Official group

Anzeigegeräte: Indicators

APMO: Archives of the Polish Museum at Oswiecim [Auschwitz]

Arginal: A gas

Aspiration: Exhaust process

Aufnahmegebäude: Admittance building

Aufzeichnungen: Notes, records

Auschwitz: German spelling for the Upper Silesian town, [Polish name Oswiecim, c. 45,000 inhabitants] located 2 km Southwest from the former large complex which is known as Auschwitz-Birkenau

Auskleidekeller: Disrobing basement

B

Badenanstalten: Swimming, bathing facilities
Baracken: Barracks
Bauhof: Construction yard
Bauleitung: Construction administration, office in charge of construction
Bavure: Trace
Behelfsmässig: Temporary, makeshift, improvised
Berücksichtigt: In consideration
Bescheinigung: Receipt, certificate
Blausäure: Hydrocyanic acid
Blausäuregaskammern: Hydrocyanic acid gas chambers
Blausäurekammern: Hydrocyanic acid chambers
Boos: Name of a German manufacturer (Friedrich Boos)
Brennstoffverbrauch: Fuel consumption
Buchenwald: Location of a German concentration camp
Bundesarchiv: German archives
Bunker: Shelter

C

Chemischtechnischer: Chemical-technical
Crypto-revisionist: Secret, or underground revisionist
Czech (Danuta): Author of *Kalendarium der Ereignisse* im Konzentrationslager Auschwitz-Birkenau 1939-1948

D

Degesch-Kreislauf: Circulatory system type Degesch
Drahtnetzeinschiebvorrichtung: Meshed-wire slider
Drahtseil: Wire rope
Dreimuffel-Einäscherungs-Öfen: Three-chambered crematory ovens
Druckluftgebläse: Compressed air blower
Druckluft-Anlage: Compressed air installation

E

Einäscherungsofen: Crematory oven
Einäscherungsverfahren: Cremation procedure
Einsatzfähigkeit: Operational capability
Einwurfvorrichtung: Insertion installation
Entlausungsbaracken: Disinfestation barracks, barracks for de-lousing
Entlüftungsanlage: Exhaust equipment
Entlüftungskanäle: Exhaust channels
Erfurt: A German city
Europaverlag: A German publishing establishment

F

Feuerbestattung: Cremation
Feuerungstechnik: Cremation techniques
Fleckfieberabwehr: Typhus prevention

G

Gasentwicklung: Gas development
Gasogene (Gazogene): An apparatus producing gas for fuel by burning coke, charcoal
or wood
Gasprüfer: Gas tester
Gasrestnachweisgeräte: Residual gas indicators (indicating instruments)
Generatorgase: Generator gases
Gestapo: Geheime Staatspolizei — Secret State Police later incorporated into the Reich Main Security Office headed by Heinrich Muller
Gesundheitspflege: Health care
Gesundheits-Ingenieur: Health engineer
Gleichschaltung: Co-ordination
Gusseisern: Wrought iron

H

Hamburg: Northern German port city
Handwinde: Hand winch

Hauptamt: Main office
Hauptfriedhof: Main cemetery
Hauptsturmführer: Captain
Häftlinge: Prisoners
HCN: Hydrocyanic acid
Heisslufteinäscherungsofen: Hot air crematory oven
Holzblenden: Wooden shutters
Holzdeckel: Wooden lid(s)
Holzgebläse: Wooden blowers
HUTA: Acronym for Hoch und Tiefbau AG (a construction firm)

J
Judenumsiedlung: Jewish resettlement

K
Kammerinhalts: Room contents
Kellerzugang: Cellar or basement entrance
KGL: Prisoner of war camp
KL: War camp
Koblenz: A German city
Koksbeheizt: Heated by coke
Koksfeuerung: Coke burner
Konzentrationslager: Concentration camp
Kori: A German manufacturer
Kostenanschlag: Cost estimate
Kostenvoranschlag: Preliminary cost estimate
Krakow: A Polish city
Kreislauf: Circulation
Kreislauf-Begasungskammern: Circulatory gas chambers
Kriegsgefangenenlager: Prisoner of war camp

L
Lagergemeinschaft: Camp community
Leicheneinäscherungsöfen: Corpse crematory ovens
Leichenhalle: Mortuary

Leichenhallenbuch: Mortuary book or register
Leichenkeller: Mortuary basement
Leichenkühlräume: Corpse cooling rooms
Leichenverbrennungsöfen: Corpse cremating ovens
Leichenverbrennungs-Anstalten: Corpse cremating faciliities
Luftwechsel: Air exchange

M
Miasma: Noxious
Militärärztliche: Of a military physician nature

N
Nazi: Acronym for Nationalsozialistische (National Socialist)
Nord-süd: North-South

O
Obergruppenführer: The rank of General
Ofenanlage: Oven installation
Offenbach: A German city
Öfen: Ovens
Öffentlich: Public
Österreichisch: Austrian

P
Planrost: Level grate
Politruks: Soviet political officers charged with a number of functions among the troops, including political supervision and agitation. Commonly translated as "Commissars"
POWs: Prisoners of war
Propaganda: Any organized movement to spread particular doctrines, information, etc.

R
Rauchgasanalyse: Smoke gas analysis

Rauchkanalschieber: Smoke channel slider (control mechanism)

Refractory: Fire retardant or resistant

Reichsarbeitblatt: German government worksheet

Reichsführer: Reich leader. Position occupied by Heinrich Himmler from 1929 to 1945

Reichsmark: The traditional German monetary unit

Revisionists: Those who look back again in order to correct or improve

RM: Reichsmark

RSHA: Reichssicherkeitshauptamt. Reich Main Security Office formed in 1939. Departments: Intelligence, Gestapo, Criminal Police and the SD (Sicherheitsdienst)

S

Sach-Entlausung: Material delousing

Saugzuganlage: Exhaust installation

Schädlingsbekämpfung: Pest control

Schlachtfeld: Battlefield

Schmiedeeisengebläse: Wrought-iron blower

Schornsteinfutter: Chimney casing

SD: Sicherheitsdienst, Security Service

Sonder: Out of the ordinary routine

Sonderbaumassnahmen: Special construction and building, undertaking and procedures

Sondermassnahmen: Special undertaking and procedures

Sonderveröffentlichung: Special publication

SS: Schutzstaffel, protective echelon

SS-Neubauleitung: SS Ofice for new construction

SS-Obersturmführer: The rank of Lieutenant

SS-Sturmbannführer: The rank of Major

SS-WVHA: SS Wirtschaftsverwaltungshauptamt, Central Office of the SS Economic Administration

Staatsarchiv: State archives

Stammlager: Original camp (Auschwitz) "Central

Camp"
Sterbebücher: Death records
Sturmbannführer: The rank of Major

T

Tagelohn-Arbeiten: Part-time work
Taschenbuch: Pocket book (notebook)
Tesch: Bruno Tesch, engineer
Testa: Acronym for Tesch und Stabenow, German
    engineering firm
Topf: A German engineering and manufacturing firm
Topf-Doppelmuffel-Einäscherungs-Ofen: Topf two-
    chambered crematory oven
Topf-Zugverstärkungs-Anlage: Topf facility for
    increased circulation

U

Übergabeverhandlung: Transfer negotiations or pro-
    ceedings of transfer

V

Verhältnismässig: In relation to
VL-Kremationsofen: A crematory oven type built by
    the firm Volckmann-Ludwig

W

Wärmebilanz: Heat balance
Wärmewirtschaft: Heat distribution
WVHA: WirtschaftsVerwaltungshauptamt (Central
    Office of Economic Administration)

Z

Zyklon B: Cyclon B chemical disinfectant

Index

F

Flury, Ferdinand, 39
Freund, Florian, 46
Frickhinger, H. W., 71
Fritzsch, 35
Frölich, H., 94

G

Glowacki, 39
Gusen, 11, 23, 30, 94, 96, 108

H

Heepke, Wilhelm, 22, 94, 114
Heinicke, H. R., 93
Helwig, Friedrich, 93
Hermsdorf, A., 106
Himmler, Heinrich, 25, 34, 35, 36, 37, 41, 42, 43, 72
Höss, Rudolf, 27, 34, 36, 37, 38, 44, 72, 74, 76, 95

J

Jährling, 69, 71
Jakobskötter, R., 30, 96
Jones, E. W., 92
Jothann, Werner, 3

K

Kamper, Herman, 93
Kessler, Richard, 17, 23, 93, 108
Kielar, 39
Klodzinski, S., 38, 97
Kori, H., 12, 92
Kremer, Johann Paul, 50
Kremer, Tibere, 101
Kula, M., 38

L

Langbein, Hermann, 94

Lenzer, 92
Leuchter Report, 100
Lublin, 12

M

Majdanek, 64
Marsalek, H., 96
Mauthausen, 9, 10, 92, 94, 96
Mildner, 97
Müller, Filip, 109

N

Nyiszli, Miklos, 78, 101

P

Perz, Bertrand, 46
Peters, G., 71, 73, 75, 97, 99, 115
Piper, Franciszek, 29, 95
Pohl, Oswald, 50, 51
Prüfer, Kurt, 9, 10, 12, 23, 54, 84, 93
Puntigam, Franz, 100, 116

R

Rasch, W., 97

S

Schnabel, R., 18, 94
Schultze, Karl, 86, 87
Sehn, Jan, 97
Sieverts, A., 106
Struthof, 64
Stuhlpfaffer, Karl, 46

T

Tauber, H., 14, 15, 58, 92
Topf, Ernst-Wolfgang, 12
Topf, Ludwig, 12